DEATH OF
A SALESMAN

BY ARTHUR MILLER

★

★

DRAMATISTS
PLAY SERVICE
INC.

DEATH OF A SALESMAN was produced for the first time at the Morosco Theatre, New York, February 10, 1949. Following is the program:

KERMIT BLOOMGARDEN AND WALTER FRIED

present

Elia Kazan's Production of

DEATH OF A SALESMAN

A New Play by ARTHUR MILLER
Directed by ELIA KAZAN
Setting and Lighting by JO MIELZINER
Incidental Music Composed by ALEX NORTH
Costumes by JULIA SZE
Production Assistant DEL HUGHES

WILLY LOMAN	Lee J. Cobb
LINDA	Mildred Dunnock
HAPPY	Cameron Mitchell
BIFF	Arthur Kennedy
BERNARD	Don Keefer
THE WOMAN	Winnifred Cushing
CHARLEY	Howard Smith
UNCLE BEN	Thomas Chalmers
HOWARD WAGNER	Alan Hewitt
JENNY	Ann Driscoll
STANLEY	Tom Pedi
MISS FORSYTHE	Constance Ford
LETTA	Hope Cameron

NOTE ON THE MUSIC AND SETTING

The music for this play was especially composed by Alex North. While it is possible to produce the play without this music, this is considered highly inadvisable by those best qualified to judge. The music which runs through a good deal of the play is an integral part of the mood aimed at by the author and its use in any production adds greatly to the over-all effect. The present acting version includes all the music cues. The cassette which is clearly marked in conformity with the cues in the script, may be secured from the Dramatists Play Service for a fee. While purchase of the music gives the buyer the right to possess it, attention is called to the fact that possession does not include the right to use it or any parts of it in connection with a production of the play. Any non-professional group authorized to give a production may use the music on payment to the Service five days before the play's opening.

On one of the music selections, which is to be used (according to the proper cue) in the scene where Willy is to be hit by the car (Music Cue No. 16-A), please note that just a second before the No. 16-A music starts, there is the sound of a car door slamming offstage. The actual sound of a car starting, and pulling away, may be added to the offstage effect noted here, or the discordant music may be used alone instead of the actual car sounds. This point may be wisely left to the judgment of the director. It all depends on the over-all effect created up to this point in the play. Perhaps a good idea might be to use the car starting up and pulling away synchronously with Music Cue No. 16-A. At all events, the music should be used.

The frontispiece photo showing the set, it should be noted, differs slightly from the description of the set in stage directions on page 5. The director should take special notice of the discrepancies. Instead of two beds in the boys' bedroom there is only one, a double-decker. Instead of the stairway from the boys' bedroom coming down on the stage to the left, it comes down to the right. The master bedroom downstairs is shown in the photo on a raised platform. The stage directions eliminate all mention of the platform. The refrigerator is shown in the photo as being center instead of left. Finally, the curtains shown in the up center kitchen wall should be omitted.

4

DEATH OF A SALESMAN

ACT I

*Music is heard before the rise of the curtain. MUSIC
CUE NO. 1. During the music, shortly after it begins,
the curtain goes up. Before us, at first only partly visible,
is the Salesman's house. We are aware of towering,
angular shapes behind it, surrounding it on all sides.
Only the blue light of the sky falls upon the house and
forestage; the surrounding area shows an angry glow of
orange. As more appears, we see a solid vault of apartment houses around the small, fragile-seeming home. An
air of the dream clings to the place, a dream rising out
of reality. The kitchen seems actual enough. To the R. of
the kitchen is a draped entrance to a bedroom furnished
only with a brass bedstead and a straight chair. Behind
the kitchen, at an elevation of about six and a half feet,
is the Boys' Bedroom, at first barely visible. The double
bunk is dimly seen. Leading down to the kitchen below
are three or four stairs. The entire setting is wholly or—
in some places—partially transparent. The roofline of the
house is one-dimensional; under and over it we see the
apartment buildings. Before the house lies an apron—
i. e. the stage proper—curving beyond the forestage toward and down to the orchestra. This forward area
serves as a back yard as well as a locale of all WILLY'S
imaginings and of his city scenes. Whenever the action
is in the present the actors observe the imaginary wall-
lines, entering the house only through its door at the L.,
which leads into the kitchen. But in the scenes of the
past these boundaries are broken, and the actors enter
and leave a room by stepping " through a wall " onto the
forestage. It is to be noted that two exits from the set
are provided for use during dimouts or blackouts between the scenes, allowing the actors to slip out of the*

Boys' Bedroom downstairs at the upper part of the set, and the other at the upper part of the Bathroom, through the "split curtain." All necessary details of the set are provided in the stage directions, and the stage plan, on p. 104. Throughout the play lighting is a necessary part of the production. The lighting effects are used to some extent to provide atmosphere and mood, but more particularly to focus the audience's attention on those parts of the stage where each scene passes. Each of these scenes—including those "realistic" scenes that pass in the house and are of the present time and the dream or memory scenes that are set outside the house itself—requires lights that concentrate upon one room or part of a room, while the rest of the stage is not lighted, or at least only partly lighted. In some of the dream scenes, where no particular realistic background is required and only one character appears (as in some of the scenes with THE WOMAN), only a single spot is called for. In view of what has just been said, it is considered unnecessary to indicate light cues hereafter. Invariably the lights go down or out when the action ceases in one scene, and up on the next scene.

Shortly after the curtain rises the Salesman—WILLY LOMAN—slowly walks into the light from stage R. He is dressed in a dark gray business suit, felt hat under his arm, and carries two large sample cases. He is very tired, very confused. A flute is heard in the distance, soft, beguiling, memorable. He hears it but is not aware of it. It plays a tiny melody of grass and trees and the horizon. WILLY is sixty now, a man of powerful strivings and the images that possess. His emotions, in a word, are mercurial. He crosses stage L., unlocks door and enters kitchen. He puts cases down and sighs—they are heavy. He feels callouses on his hand, slams door. In bedroom—"Master Bedroom"—LINDA sits up, fumbles for a robe, and puts it and slippers on. WILLY is in kitchen. He takes hat from under his arm, catching his breath, then rubs his hand over his face, shaking his head. . . .

WILLY. Oh boy, oh boy! (*He just stands there, staring, half a wondrous smile on his face. He keeps shaking his head ever so little in exhaustion. Now turns, takes a breath, picks up his bags and walks* R*., puts bags inside entrance to bedroom.* LINDA *has been asleep in bed. Most often jovial, she has developed an iron repression of her objections to him. Her struggle is to spiritually support him while trying to insinuate guidance and her superior and calmer intelligence.*)

LINDA. (*Sitting on bed.*) Willy!

WILLY. · (*Still in doorway to bedroom.*) It's all right, I came back.

LINDA. (*Getting up.*) Why? What happened? (*Slight pause.*) Did something happen, Willy?

WILLY. No, nothing happened.

LINDA. You didn't smash the car, did you?

WILLY. (*With casual irritation.*) I said nothing happened. Didn't you hear me?

LINDA. (*Crossing* U.) Don't you feel well?

WILLY. (*Enters bedroom.*) I'm tired to the death. (*Music fades out.* WILLY *crosses* D*., sits on chair opposite* C. *of bed. Slight pause.*) I couldn't make it. I just couldn't make it, Linda.

LINDA. (*At his* R*., very carefully, delicately.*) Where were you all day? You look terrible.

WILLY. I got as far as a little above Yonkers. I stopped for a cup of coffee. . . . Maybe it was the coffee.

LINDA. What?

WILLY. (*Pause—bewildered.*) I suddenly couldn't drive any more. The car kept going off onto the shoulder, y' know?

LINDA. (*Helpfully. Taking off his coat.*) Oh. . . . Maybe it's the steering again. I don't think Angelo knows the Studebaker.

WILLY. No, it's me, it's me. Suddenly I'm goin' sixty miles an hour and I don't remember driving the last five minutes. I'm . . . I can't seem to . . . keep my mind to it.

LINDA. Maybe it's your glasses. You never went for your new glasses.

WILLY. No, I see everything. I came back ten miles an hour. It took me nearly four hours from Yonkers.

LINDA. (*Resigned.*) Well, you'll just have to take a rest, Willy, you can't continue this way. (*Puts his coat on bed.*)

WILLY. I just got back from Florida. (*Starts taking off shoes.*)

LINDA. (*Helping with his shoes.*) But you didn't rest your mind.

7

Your mind is overactive, and the mind is what counts, dear.

WILLY. I'll start out in the morning. Maybe I'll feel better in the morning. (*She puts on his slippers.*) These goddam arch supports are killing me.

LINDA. Take an aspirin. Should I get you an aspirin? (*Starts up toward bathroom U.*) It'll soothe you.

WILLY. (*Stops her. Puts his R. arm around her shoulder as she kneels at his R. knee. With wonder.*) I was driving along, you understand? And I was fine. I was even observing the scenery. You can imagine, me looking at scenery, on the road every week of my life! But it's so beautiful up there, Linda, the trees are so thick, and the sun is warm. . . . I opened the windshield and just let the warm air bathe over me. And then all of a sudden I'm goin' off the road. . . . I'm tellin' ya, I absolutely forgot I was driving. If I'd've gone the other way over the white line I might've killed somebody. So I went on again . . . and five minutes later I'm dreamin' again, and I nearly . . . (*Presses two fingers against his eyes.*) I have such thoughts, I have such strange thoughts. (*Rises, crosses U.*)

LINDA. (*Quickly follows after him.*) Willy, dear. Talk to them again. There's no reason why you can't work in New York.

WILLY. (*Proud.*) They don't need me in New York. I'm the New England man. I'm vital in New England.

LINDA. (*Comforting him.*) But you're sixty years old. They can't expect you to keep traveling every week.

WILLY. I'll have to send a wire to Portland—I'm supposed to see Brown and Morrison tomorrow morning at ten o'clock to show the line. Goddamit, I could sell them! (*Crosses D. to middle of bed, puts arm in sleeve of coat.*)

LINDA. (*Crosses D., gently stops his putting coat on.*) Why don't you go down to the place tomorrow and tell Howard you've simply got to work in New York? You're too accommodating, dear.

WILLY. If old Frank Wagner was alive I'd 'a' been in charge of New York now! That man was a prince, he was a masterful man. But that boy of his, that Howard, he don't appreciate. When I went north the first time, the Wagner Company didn't know where New England was!

LINDA. (*Taking his coat off. Not arguing.*) Why don't you tell those things to Howard, dear?

WILLY. (*Encouraged.*) I will, I definitely will. . . . Is there any cheese?

LINDA. I'll make you a sandwich.

WILLY. No, go to sleep. I'll take some milk. (*Crosses into bathroom.* LINDA *sits on bed, looking at torn lining in coat.*) I'll be up right away. (*Crosses back in.*) The boys in?

LINDA. (*Happily.*) They're sleeping. Happy took Biff on a date tonight.

WILLY. (*Interested.*) That so?

LINDA.· It was so nice to see them shaving together, one behind the other in the bathroom. And going out together . . . you notice? —the whole house smells of shaving lotion.

WILLY. (*Crosses* L. *to* U. S.) Figure it out; work a lifetime to pay off a house. You finally own it, and there's nobody to live in it.

LINDA. Well, dear, life is a casting-off, it's always that way.

WILLY. (*Crosses* D. 2 *steps.*) No, no, some people . . . some people accomplish something. Did Biff say anything after I went this morning?

LINDA. (*Gently.*) You shouldn't have criticized him, Willy, especially after he just got off the train. You mustn't lose your temper with him.

WILLY. (*Crossing* D. *to her.*) When the hell did I lose my temper? I simply asked him if he was making any money. Is that a criticism?

LINDA. (*Takes his* R. *hand.*) But, dear, how could he make any money?

WILLY. (*Worried, angered. Takes hand away.*) There's such an undercurrent in him. (*Crossing* U.) He became a moody man. Did he apologize when I left this morning? (*Turns back.*)

LINDA. He was crestfallen, Willy. You know how he admires you. I think if he finds himself, then you'll both be happier and not fight any more.

WILLY. (*Crosses* D., *sits on chair.*) How can he find himself on a farm? Is that a life? A farmhand? In the beginning, when he was young, I thought well, a young man—it's good for him to tramp around, take a lot of different jobs. But it's more than ten years now and he has yet to make thirty-five dollars a week!

LINDA. He's finding himself, Willy.

WILLY. (*Rises.*) Not finding yourself at the age of thirty-four is a disgrace!

9

LINDA. (*Rises.*) Sshh!

WILLY. The trouble is he's lazy, goddammit!

LINDA. Willy, please!

WILLY. Biff is a lazy bum!

LINDA. They're sleeping. Get something to eat. Go on down.

WILLY. Why did he come home? I would like to know what brought him home.

LINDA. I don't know. I think he's still lost, Willy. I think he's very lost.

WILLY. Biff Loman is lost. In the greatest country in the world a young man with such . . . personal attractiveness, gets lost. . . . And such a hard worker! There's one thing about Biff—he's not lazy.

LINDA. Never.

WILLY. (*Now with pity and resolve.*) I'll see him in the morning; I'll have a nice talk with him. I'll get him a job selling. He could be big in no time. (*Starts to exit, then returns.* LINDA *sits on bed, puts hair up with hairpins she gets from under pillow.*) My God . . . remember how they used to follow him around in high school? (*Crosses D. slowly to D. S. edge of bedroom.*) When he smiled at one of them their faces lit up. When he walked down the street . . . (*Hits fist into his hand in desperation. He is lost in reminiscing, and* LINDA *tries to bring him out of it.*)

LINDA. (*Rises, crosses D. to his L. Shaking his L. arm gently.*) Willy, dear, I got a new kind of American type cheese today. It's whipped.

WILLY. Why do you get American when I like Swiss?

LINDA. I just thought you'd like a change. . . .

WILLY. I don't want a change! I want Swiss cheese. Why am I always being contradicted?

LINDA. (*With covering laugh.*) I thought it would be a surprise.

WILLY. Why don't you open a window in here, for God's sake?

LINDA. (*With infinite patience.*) They're all open, dear.

WILLY. The way they boxed us in here. Bricks and windows, windows and bricks.

LINDA. (*Not criticizing.*) We should've bought the land next door. . . .

WILLY. The street is lined with cars. (*Loosens collar and tie. Sits on bed.*) There's not a breath of fresh air in the neighborhood. The grass don't grow any more, you can't raise a carrot in the

10

back yard. (LINDA *kneels on bed above him, strokes his temples.*) They should've had a law against apartment houses. Remember those two beautiful elm trees out there? When I and Biff hung the swing between them?

LINDA. (*Sits on bed.*) Yeah, like being a million miles from the city.

WILLY. They should've arrested the builder for cutting those down. They massacred the neighborhood. (*Lost. Longing.*) More and more I think of those days, Linda. This time of year it was lilac and wisteria. And then the peonies would come out, and the daffodils. What fragrance in this room!

LINDA. Well, after all, people had to move somewhere.

WILLY. No, there's more people now.

LINDA. I don't think there's more people. I think . . .

WILLY. (*Rises. Crossing u. shouting.*) There's more people! That's what's ruining this country! (HAPPY, *in double bunk in Boys' Bedroom, wakes up.*) Population is getting out of control. The competition is maddening! Smell the stink from that apartment house! (BIFF, *also in double bunk, lifts his head.*) And another one on the other side . . . (*Suddenly* WILLY *realizes he is shaking.*) How can they whip cheese?

LINDA. (*Rises, crosses u. to him.*) Go now and try it. And be quiet.

WILLY. (*Turns in guilt.*) You're not worried about me, are you, sweetheart?

LINDA. You've got too much on the ball to worry about.

WILLY. (*Strokes her hair.*) You're my foundation and my support, Linda.

LINDA. (*As he hugs her.*) Just try to relax, dear. You make mountains out of molehills. (BIFF *puts his head down again.*)

WILLY. I won't fight with him any more. If he wants to go back to Texas, let him go.

LINDA. He'll find his way.

WILLY. Sure. Certain men just don't get started till later in life. Like Thomas Edison, I think. Or B. F. Goodrich. . . . One of them was deaf. (*Starting out* L.) I'll put my money on Biff. . . .

HAPPY. (*Rises. Crosses* L. *He has on red button neck pajamas. Then crosses u. Takes cigarette and matches from pajama pocket.*) Biff, I think Pop is back.

LINDA. And, Willy . . . if it's warm Sunday we'll drive in the country. And we'll open the windshield, and take lunch . . .

11

WILLY. (*Playfully.*) No, the windshields don't open on the new cars.

LINDA. But you opened it today.

WILLY. Me? I didn't . . . (*He stops.*) Now isn't that peculiar! (*Music of the flute is heard. MUSIC CUE NO. 2.*) Isn't that remarkable. . . . (*He breaks off in amazement and fright. HAPPY, at Boys' Bedroom wall with back to audience, lights cigarette.*)

LINDA. What, darling?

WILLY. That is the most remarkable thing.

LINDA. What, dear?

WILLY. I was thinking of the Chevy. (*Slight pause.*) 1928 . . . when I had that red Chevy . . . (*Breaks off.*) That funny? I coulda sworn I was driving that Chevy today. (*BIFF gets up from bunk, crosses D. facing front, listening. BIFF is wearing light bluish gray button neck pajamas.*)

LINDA. Well, that's *nothing.* Something must've reminded you.

WILLY. Remarkable. Tch! Remember those days?—the way Biff used to simonize that car? The dealer refused to believe there was eighty thousand miles on it. (*Shakes head.*) Heh. (*Now to her.*) Close your eyes, I'll be right up. (*He is walking into kitchen. Music fades out.*)

HAPPY. (*In Boys' Bedroom, to BIFF at R. of him.*) Jesus, maybe he smashed up the car again!

LINDA. (*Calling after WILLY who is going into kitchen.*) Be careful on the stairs, dear! The cheese is on the middle shelf! (*She turns, comes down to his coat on the bed. WILLY starts out of bedroom, goes to kitchen—talking to himself. BIFF comes downstage a bit and stands attentively. He is two years older than his brother, HAPPY, well-built but in these days bears a worn air, and seems less self-assured. He has succeeded less, and his dreams are stronger and less acceptable than HAPPY'S. HAPPY is tall, powerfully made. Sexuality is like a visible color on him, or a scent that many women have discovered. He, like his brother, is lost, but in a different way, for he has never allowed himself to turn his face toward defeat and is thus more confused and hardskinned, although seemingly happier. Both BIFF and HAPPY are under-dressed.*)

HAPPY. He's going to get his license taken away if he keeps that up. I'm getting nervous about him, y' know, Biff?

BIFF. His eyes are going.

HAPPY. No, I've driven with him. He sees all right. He just doesn't keep his mind on it. I drove into the city with him last week. He stops at a green light and then it turns red and he goes. (*Laughs.*)

BIFF. Maybe he's color-blind!

HAPPY. Pop? Why, he's got the finest eye for color in the business. You know that.

BIFF. I'm going to sleep. (*Fixes bed.*)

HAPPY. You're not still sour on Dad, are you, Biff?

BIFF. He's all right, I guess. (*Starts* U.)

WILLY. (*Pacing in kitchen. Unfastens collar and tie.* BIFF *stops, listens:*) Yes, sir, eighty thousand miles . . . eighty-two thousand!

BIFF. You smoking?

HAPPY. Want one? (*Offers* BIFF *his lighted cigarette.*)

BIFF. (*Taking it, crossing* R., *sits chair.*) I can never sleep when I smell it.

WILLY. (*In kitchen.*) What a simonizing job, heh! (*Exits out kitchen door* L.)

HAPPY. (*With deep sentiment.*) Funny, Biff, y'know?—us sleeping in here again? The old beds. All the talk that went across those two beds, huh? Our whole lives.

BIFF. Yeah . . . lotta dreams and plans.

HAPPY. (*With a laugh, deep and masculine.*) About five hundred women would like to know what was said in this room! (*They share a soft laugh.*)

BIFF. Remember that big Betsy something—what the hell was her name, over on Bushwick Avenue?

HAPPY. With the collie dog!

BIFF. That's the one. I got you in there, remember? (*Both laugh.*)

HAPPY. Yeah, that was my first time—(*Crosses* U. L., *turns.*) I think. (*Combs hair.*) Boy, there was a pig! (*They laugh, almost crudely.* LINDA *takes* WILLY'S *coat, exits from bedroom.*) You taught me everything I know about women. Don't forget that.

BIFF. I bet you forgot how bashful you used to be. Especially with girls.

HAPPY. Oh, I still am, Biff. . . .

BIFF. Oh, go on!

HAPPY. (*Crossing* D. *to* L. *of* BIFF.) I just control it, that's all. I think I got less bashful and you got more so. What happened, Biff? (*Sits, above* BIFF, *puts arm around him.*) Where's the old humor, the old confidence? (BIFF *rises, crosses* L. *to above chest, puts cigarette out in small can on floor above chest.*) What's the matter?

BIFF. Why does Dad mock me all the time?

HAPPY. He's not mocking you, he . . .

BIFF. Everything I say there's a twist of mockery on his face. I can't get near him.

HAPPY. He just wants you to make good, that's all. I wanted to talk to you about Dad for a long time, Biff. Something's happening to him. He . . . talks to himself.

BIFF. I noticed that this morning. But he always mumbled.

HAPPY. But not so noticeable. It got so embarrassing. I sent him to Florida. And you know something? Most of the time he's talking to you.

BIFF. What's he say about me?

HAPPY. I can't make it out.

BIFF. What's he say about me?

HAPPY. (*Crosses, kneels on* BIFF'S *bed.*) I think the fact that you're not settled, that you're still kind of up in the air . . .

BIFF. There's one or two other things depressing him, Happy.

HAPPY. What do you mean?

BIFF. Never mind. Just don't lay it all to me.

HAPPY. But I think if you just got started . . . I mean . . . is there any future for you out there?

BIFF. I tell ya, Hap . . . I don't know what the future is; I don't know . . . what I'm supposed to want.

HAPPY. (*Sits chair.*) What do you mean?

BIFF. (*With frustration.*) Well, I spent six or seven years after high school trying to work myself up. Shipping clerk, salesman, business of one kind or another . . . and it's a measly manner of existence. To get on that subway on the hot mornings in summer; to devote your whole life to keeping stock, or making phone calls, or selling or buying. . . . To suffer fifty weeks of the year for the sake of a two-week vacation, when all you really desire is to be outdoors, with your shirt off. And always to have to get ahead of the next fella. . . . And still . . . that's how you build a future.

HAPPY. Well, you really enjoy it on a farm? Are you content out there?

BIFF. (*With rising agitation. Kneeling above chest, and looking at athletic equipment in it. Finally finds old deflated football, puts other things back.*) Hap, I've had twenty or thirty different kinds of jobs since I left home before the war, and it always turns out the same. I just realized it lately. In Nebraska when I herded cattle, and the Dakotas, and Arizona, and now in Texas. It's why I came home now, I guess, because I realized it—this farm I work on, it's spring there now, see. And they've got about fifteen new colts. There's nothing more inspiring or . . . beautiful, than the sight of a mare and a new colt. And it's cool there now, see? Texas is cool now, and it's spring. (*Crosses* U.) And whenever spring comes to where I am, I suddenly get the feeling —— My God (*Crosses* D.), I'm not gettin' anywhere! (*Crosses* U.) What the hell am I doing, playing around with horses, twenty-eight dollars a week! (*Crosses* D., *to himself.*) I'm thirty-four years old, I oughta be makin' my future. That's when I come running home. And now—I get here, and I don't know what to do with myself. (*Pause.*) I've always made a point of not wasting my life, and every time I come back here I know that all I've done is to waste my life. (*Throws football into chest.*)

HAPPY. (*Awed.*) You're a poet, you know that, Biff? You're a . . . you're an idealist!

BIFF. No, I'm mixed up very bad. (BIFF *closes chest cover.*) Maybe I oughta get married. Maybe I oughta get stuck into something. Maybe that's my trouble. I'm like a boy . . . I'm not married, I'm not in business, I just . . . I'm like a boy. Are you content, Hap? (*Sits on chest.*) You're a success, aren't you? Are you content?

HAPPY. Hell, no!

BIFF. Why? You're making money, aren't you?

HAPPY. All I can do now is wait for the merchandise manager to die. . . . And suppose I get to be merchandise manager? He's a good friend of mine, and he just built a terrific estate on Long Island. And he lived there about two months and sold it, and now he's building another one. He can't enjoy it once it's finished. And I know that's just what I would do. I don't know what the hell I'm workin' for. Sometimes I sit in my apartment . . . all alone. And I think of the rent I'm paying. And it's crazy. But then . . . it's what I always wanted. My own apartment, a car and plenty of women. And still, goddammit, I'm lonely.

BIFF. (*With enthusiasm.*) Listen, why don't you come out West with me?

15

HAPPY. You and I, heh?

BIFF. Sure, maybe we could buy a ranch. Raise cattle, use our muscles. Men built like we are should be working out in the open.

HAPPY. (*Avidly.*) The Loman Brothers, heh?

BIFF. (*With vast affection.*) Sure, we'd be known all over the counties!

HAPPY. (*Rises. Enthralled.*) That's what I dream about, Biff Sometimes I want to just rip my clothes off in the middle of the store and outbox that goddam merchandise manager. I mean I can outbox, outrun, and outlift anybody in that store, and I have to take orders from those common, petty sons of bitches till I can't stand it any more.

BIFF. (*Rises.*) I'm tellin' you, kid, if you were with me I'd be happy out there.

HAPPY. (*Enthused.*) See, Biff, everybody around me is so false that I'm constantly lowering my ideals. . . .

BIFF. (*More enthused.*) Baby, together we'd stand up for one another, we'd have someone to trust.

HAPPY. But if I were around you . . .

BIFF. Hap, the trouble is we weren't brought up to grub for money. I don't know how to do it . . .

HAPPY. (*Shouts.*) Neither can I!

BIFF. (*Shouts.*) Then let's go!

HAPPY. (*Subdued.*) The only thing is . . . what can you *make* out there?

BIFF. But look at your friend. Builds an estate and then hasn't the peace of mind to live in it. . . .

HAPPY. Yeah, but when he walks into the store the waves part in front of him. (BIFF *puts foot on chest.*) That's fifty-two thousand dollars a year coming through the revolving door, and I got more in my pinky than he's got in his head.

BIFF. Yeah, but . . . You just said . . .

HAPPY. I gotta show some of those pompous, self-important executives over there that Hap Loman can make the grade. I want to walk into the store the way he walks in. Then I'll go with you, Biff. We'll be together yet, I swear. But take those two creatures we had tonight. Now weren't they gorgeous?

BIFF. Yeah, yeah, most gorgeous I've had in years.

HAPPY. I get that any time I want, Biff. Whenever I feel disgusted. The only trouble is, it gets like bowling, or something—I just keep knockin' them over and it doesn't mean anything. You still run around a lot?

BIFF. Naahh. . . . I'd like to find a girl . . . steady, somebody with substance.

HAPPY. That's what I long for. . . .

BIFF. Go on. . . . You'd never come home.

HAPPY. I would! Somebody with character. Like Mom, y'know, somebody with resistance! (*Crosses R. Gets hat off hook on bedroom wall, puts it on.*) You're gonna call me a bastard when I tell you this. That girl Charlotte I was with tonight is engaged to be married in five weeks.

BIFF. No kiddin'.

HAPPY. Sure—the guy's in line for the vice-presidency of the store —— I don't know what gets into me, maybe I just have an over-developed sense of competition or something. (*Crosses L. to* BIFF. *They cross U.*) But I went and ruined her, and furthermore I can't get rid of her. And he's the third executive I've done that to. Isn't that a crummy characteristic! (*They cross D.* BIFF *starts to sit on chair.* HAPPY *takes his arm and stops him.*) And to top it all I go to their weddings! Like I'm not supposed to take bribes. Manufacturers offer me a hundred-dollar bill now and then to throw an order their way. You know how honest I am, but it's like this girl, see, I hate myself for it. Because I don't want the girl . . . and still . . . I take it and . . . I love it! (BIFF *crosses* L. HAPPY *is hurt.*) What's the matter?

BIFF. Let's go to sleep.

HAPPY. (*Crossing R., takes hat off, puts on hook.*) I guess we didn't settle anything, heh? (BIFF *crosses U., then back.*)

BIFF. I just got one idea that I think I'm going to try.

HAPPY. What's that?

BIFF. Remember Bill Oliver?

HAPPY. (*Crossing D.*) Sure, Oliver is very big now. You want to work for him again?

BIFF. No, but when I quit he said something to me. He put his arm on my shoulder, and he said, " Biff, if you ever *need* anything, come to me."

HAPPY. I remember that. That sounds good.

BIFF. I think I'll go to see him. If I could get ten thousand or even seven or eight thousand dollars I could buy a beautiful ranch.

HAPPY. I bet he'd back you. 'Cause he thought highly of you, Biff.

I mean they all do; you're well liked, Biff, that's why I say to come back here, and we both have the apartment and I'm tellin' you, Biff, any babe you want . . .

BIFF. No. With a ranch I could do the work I like and still be something. I just wonder, though . . . I wonder if Oiver still thinks I stole that carton of basketballs? (WILLY *enters kitchen through door* L.)

HAPPY. Oh, he probably forgot that long ago. It's almost ten years. You're too sensitive. Anyway, he didn't really fire you.

BIFF. Well, I think he was going to; I think that's why I quit. I was never sure whether he knew or not. I know he thought the world of me, though. I was the only one he'd let lock up the place.

WILLY. (*Calls to upstairs.*) You gonna wash the engine, Biff?

HAPPY. Ssh! (BIFF *looks at him.* HAPPY *is looking down, listening.* WILLY *is mumbling in kitchen.*) You hear that? (*They listen.* WILLY *laughs warmly.*)

BIFF. (*Growing angry.*) Doesn't he know Mom can hear that?

WILLY. Don't get your sweater dirty, Biff!

HAPPY. You hear that? Isn't that terrible? (*A look of pain comes onto* BIFF's *face.*) Don't leave again, will you? You'll find a job here. You gotta stick around. I don't know what to do about him, it's getting embarrassing . . .

WILLY. (*In kitchen.*) What a simonizing job!

BIFF. Mom's hearing that. . . .

WILLY. No kiddin', Biff, you got a date? Wonderful!

HAPPY. Go on to sleep; but talk to him in the morning, will you?

BIFF. With her in the house. Brother!

HAPPY. (*Crossing* U.) I wish you'd have a good talk with him. (WILLY *is carefree and happy. He is in his vest. His collar and tie are unfastened.*)

BIFF. That selfish, stupid . . . (*Disappears around behind bunk.*)

HAPPY. Sh. . . . Sleep, Biff. (*Following* BIFF. *Well before they have finished speaking,* WILLY's *form has been dimly seen below in darkened kitchen. He has opened refrigerator, searched in it, and taken out jar of cheese and bread.*)

WILLY. (*Making a sandwich. As boys are going to bed above.*) Just wanna be careful with those girls, Biff, that's all. Don't make any promises. No promises of any kind. Because a girl, y'know, they always believe what you tell 'em, and you're very young,

Biff, you're too young to be talking seriously to girls. (*Now boys are in bed.* WILLY *is eating sandwich in kitchen, talking, totally immersed in himself, and smiling faintly. Boys exit* R. U. *behind house and fence unseen by audience, and change clothes.* WILLY, *crossing* D. *to above kitchen table, talks to* BIFF *as though he were sitting* L. *of table.*) Too young entirely, Biff. You want to watch your schooling, first, then when you're all set, there'll be plenty of girls for a boy like you. (*Smiles broadly.*) That so, the girls pay for you? (*Laughs through this.*) Boy, you must really be makin'. a hit. (*He is gradually addressing—physically—a point offstage,* R., *speaking through wall of kitchen, and his voice has been rising in volume to that of a normal conversation.*) I been wondering why you polish the car so careful. Ha! Don't leave the hubcaps, boys . . . get that chamois to the hubcaps. Happy, use newspaper on the windows, it's the easiest thing. Show him how to do it, Biff! You see, Happy? Pad it up, use it like a pad . . . that's it, that's it, good work. You're doin' all right, Hap. (*Music fades out. There is a short pause.* WILLY *stands still. Pause. He stands, nodding with approbation for a few seconds, then looks upward off* L.) Biff, first thing we gotta do when we get time is clip that big branch over the house. Afraid it's gonna fall in a storm and hit the roof. (*Steps out of kitchen on to stage* L.) Tell you what. We get a nice rope and sling her around, and then we climb up there with a couple a saws and take her down. Soon as you finish the car. (*Calling off* R. *MUSIC CUE NO. 4.*) I got a surprise for you, boys.

BIFF. (*Off* R.) Whatta ya got, Dad?

WILLY. No, you finish first. "Never leave a job till you're finished," remember that. (*Looks off* R.) Biff, up in Albany I saw a beautiful hammock. I think I'll buy it next trip and we'll hang it right between those two elms. (*Pointing off* L.) Wouldn't that be something? Just swingin' there under those branches. Boy, that would be . . . (*Young* [1] BIFF *and young* HAPPY *appear from* D. R., *the direction* WILLY *was addressing.* HAPPY *carries a chamois and a pail of water. They indicate direction of car offstage.* BIFF *carries a football. He wears sweater with large " S " and sneakers and gray tweed slacks.* HAPPY *wears old sweatshirt, tennis shoes and old gray slacks.* WILLY *joins them.*)

---

[1] I. e., they look somewhat younger, and are dressed in different clothes.

BIFF. (*Crossing* C. *To* WILLY.) How's that, Pop, professional?

WILLY. (*Looking toward car indicated.*) Terrific. Terrific job, boys. Good work, Biff.

HAPPY. (*Who has followed* BIFF.) Where's the surprise, Pop?

WILLY. In the back seat of the car.

HAPPY. Boy! (*Runs off* R. *with pail and chamois.*)

BIFF. What is it, Dad? Tell me, what'd you buy?

WILLY. (*Hugs him and laughs as they walk in a little circle.*) Never mind, something I want you to have. . . .

BIFF. What is it, Hap?

HAPPY. (*Off* R.) It's a punching bag!

BIFF. Oh, Pop!

WILLY. It's got Gene Tunney's signature on it! (HAPPY *runs on with punching bag. Holds it up with both hands. Music fades out.*)

BIFF. Gee, how'd you know we wanted a punching bag!? (HAPPY *lies down on his back, doing bicycle exercise.*)

WILLY. (*Sparring with* BIFF.) Well, it's the finest thing for the timing.

HAPPY. (*On his back, pedalling.*) I'm losing weight, you notice, Pop?

WILLY. (*To* HAPPY.) Jumping rope is good, too. (HAPPY *stops exercise.*)

BIFF. Did you see the new football I got?

WILLY. (*At* C.) Where'd you get a new ball?

BIFF. (*Crossing* L., *feints passing.*) The coach told me to practice my passing.

WILLY. (*Crosses* L. *to him.*) That so? And he gave you the ball, heh?

BIFF. Well, I borrowed it from the locker room. (*Laughs confidentially.*)

WILLY. (*Laughing with him at notion of the theft.*) I want you to return that.

HAPPY. (*Tagging along behind* WILLY.) I told you he wouldn't like it. (*Gets up.*)

BIFF. (*Angered.*) Well, I'm bringing it back!

WILLY. (*Cuts in. To* HAPPY.) Sure, he's gotta practice with a regulation ball, doesn't he? (*To* BIFF.) Coach'll probably congratulate you on your initiative!

BIFF. Oh, he keeps congratulating my initiative all the time, Pop.

WILLY. That's because he likes you. If somebody else took that ball there'd be an uproar. So what's the report, boys, what's the report? (*Puts arms around their shoulders and all cross* D.)

BIFF. Where'd you go this time, Dad? Gee, we were lonesome for you.

WILLY. (*Rumpling* BIFF'S *hair. Pleased.*) Lonesome, heh?

BIFF. Missed you every minute.

WILLY. Don't say! Tell you a secret, boys; don't breathe it to a soul. Some day I'll have my own business, and I'll never have to leave home any more.

HAPPY: Like Uncle Charley, heh?

WILLY. Bigger than Uncle Charley! Because Uncle Charley is not . . . liked. He's liked, but he's not . . . well liked.

BIFF.˙Where'd you go this time, Dad? (HAPPY *flops down on his stomach,* D. L. C. BIFF *squats above and a little* L. *of him.*)

WILLY. (*Crosses* U. R. C.) Well, I got on the road, and I went north to Providence. Met the Mayor.

BIFF. (*Rises, awed.*) The Mayor of Providence!

WILLY. He was sitting in the hotel lobby.

BIFF. (*Squatting on football.*) What'd he say?

WILLY. He said, "Morning!" And I said, "You got a fine city here, Mayor." And then he had a cup of coffee with me. And then I went to Waterbury. Waterbury is a fine city. Big clock city, the famous Waterbury clock. Sold a nice bill there. And then Boston — Boston is the cradle of the Revolution. A fine city. (*Crosses, sits* D.C.) And a couple of other towns in Mass., and on to Portland and Bangor and straight home!

BIFF. (*Crossing* R. *a little.*) Gee, I'd love to go with you some time, Dad.

WILLY. Soon as summer comes. . . .

HAPPY. Promise?

WILLY. You and Hap and I, and I'll show you all the towns. America is full of beautiful towns and fine, upstanding people. And they know me, boys, they know me up and down New England. The finest people. And when I bring you fellas up, there'll be open sesame for all of us, 'cause one thing, boys; I have friends. I can park my car in any street in New England, and the cops protect it like their own. This summer, heh? (*All rise.*)

BOYS. Yeah! You bet!

WILLY. We'll take our bathing suits . . .

21

HAPPY. (*Crossing* R. *to* WILLY.) We'll carry your bags, Pop! (BIFF *crosses to over* L., *practices football formations.*)

WILLY. (*Crossing* R.) Oh, won't that be something!—me comin' into the Boston stores with you boys carryin' my bags. What a sensation! (*Sees* BIFF *over* L.) You nervous, Biff, about the game?

BIFF. Not if you're gonna be there.

WILLY. (*A little* R. *of* C.) What do they say about you in school now that they made you captain?

HAPPY. (*Above and* L. *of* WILLY.) There's a crowd of girls behind him every time the classes change.

BIFF. (*Crosses* R. *to them.*) This Saturday, Pop, this Saturday . . . just for you, I'm going to break through for a touchdown.

HAPPY. You're supposed to pass.

BIFF. I'm takin' one play for Pop. (*To* WILLY.) You watch me, Pop, and when I take off my helmet that means I'm breakin' out. Then you watch me crash through that line! (*Charges* R. *between them.*)

WILLY. Oh, wait'll' I tell this in Boston! (HAPPY *puts punching bag down.* BIFF *tosses football to* HAPPY, *who centers over it, passes it to* BIFF, *then runs over* L. *as though to receive a pass from* BIFF, *who has faded back over* R., *just as* BERNARD *enters from* D. L. BERNARD *wears light brown sweater and brown corduroy pants—knee length.*)

BERNARD. (*Stops* L. *of* HAPPY. BIFF *halts over* R. HAPPY *stops over* L.) Biff, where are you? You're supposed to study with me today.

WILLY. (*At* R. C.) Hey, looka Bernard! What're you lookin' so anemic about, Bernard?

BERNARD. He's *gotta study,* Uncle Willy, he's got *Regents* next week.

HAPPY. (*Showing off for* WILLY. *Crosses* L. *to* BERNARD; *tauntingly.*) Let's box, Bernard!

BERNARD. Look out! (*Dodging to over* R. *to* BIFF. *Getting away from* HAPPY.) Listen, Biff, I heard Mr. Birnbaum say that if you don't start studyin' Math he's gonna flunk you and you won't graduate. I heard him!

WILLY. (*Hitting* BERNARD *on rear.*) You better study with him, Biff. Go ahead now.

BERNARD. (*Crosses* R. *to* R. *and behind* BIFF.) I heard him!

BIFF. (*Crosses* D. C. *Sits.*) Oh, Pop, you didn't see my sneakers!

22

(*Holds up a foot for* WILLY. HAPPY *crosses to* C. BERNARD *crosses above them, then* D. *to their* L.)

WILLY. Hey, that's a beautiful job of printing.

BERNARD. (*Wiping his glasses on sweater. Laying down the law.*) Just because he printed University of Virginia on his sneakers doesn't mean they've got to graduate him, Uncle Willy!

WILLY. (*Angered. They all cross after him, boys ad libbing.*) What're you talking about? With scholarships to three universities they're gonna flunk him?

BERNARD. (*Backing away to* L.) But I heard Mr. Birnbaum say . . .

WILLY. Don't be a pest, Bernard! (BERNARD *exits. To boys.*) What an anemic! (BERNARD *re-enters.*)

BERNARD. (*Crossing in to* R. *of* WILLY.) Okay, I'm waiting for you in my house, Biff. (*He goes out. They laugh together.*)

WILLY. (*At* L. *of group.* D. L.) Bernard is not well liked, is he?

BIFF. (*At* R. *of* HAPPY.) He's liked, but he's not well liked.

HAPPY. (*Between* BIFF *and* WILLY.) That's right, Pop.

WILLY. (*Sincerely, as all slowly cross* R. *to* D. R. BIFF *above* WILLY, HAPPY *tagging along below* WILLY.) That's just what I mean. Bernard can get the best marks in school, y' understand, but when he gets out in the business world, y' understand, you are going to be five times ahead of him. That's why I thank Almighty God you're both built like Adonises. Because the man who makes an appearance in the business world, " the man who creates personal interest, is the man who gets ahead." Be liked and you will never want. You take me, for instance; I never have to wait in line to see a buyer. " Willy Loman is here! " That's all they have to know, and I go right through.

BIFF. Did you knock them dead, Pop?

WILLY. Knocked 'em cold in Providence, slaughtered them in Boston. (HAPPY *lies on his back, doing bicycle exercises.*)

HAPPY. I'm losing weight, you notice, Pop? (LINDA *enters from behind house* U. L., *a rose rayon-cotton print house dress and apron on, a ribbon in her hair, carrying a basket of washing.*)

LINDA. (*With great energy, youth.*) Hello, dear! (*Crossing* D. *to* L. C.)

WILLY. (*Crossing to* R. C.) Sweetheart!!

LINDA. How'd the Chevy run?

WILLY. Chevrolet, Linda, is the greatest car ever built. Marvelous.

23

(*To boys.*) Since when do you let your mother carry wash up the stairs?

BIFF. Grab hold there, boy! (*Hits* HAPPY *on the rear.* HAPPY *picks up punching bag as he runs* L.)

HAPPY. Where to, Mom? (*Takes basket, crosses* L. *to below porch outside kitchen door* L.)

LINDA. Hang them up on the line. (*Crossing* R. *to* WILLY.) And you better go down to your friends, Biff. The cellar is full of boys, they don't know what to do with themselves.

BIFF. Ah, when Pop comes home they can wait! (WILLY *laughs appreciatively.*)

WILLY. You better go down and tell them what to do, Biff.

BIFF. I think I'll have them sweep out the furnace room . . . ?

WILLY. Good work, Biff.

BIFF. (*Goes directly into* C. *of kitchen and calls* U. S.) Fellas! Everybody sweep out the furnace room! I'll be right down!

VOICES. (*Off* U. L.) "All right!" "Okay, Biff."

BIFF. George and Sam and Frank, come out back, we're hangin' up the wash! Come on, Hap, on the double! (*Crosses* D., *lines up behind* HAPPY. *Both say "Hup, Hup" as* HAPPY *carrying out basket and* BIFF *carrying football, run out up behind house.*)

LINDA. (*Crossing* L. *Looking after them.*) The way they obey him!

WILLY. Well, that's training, the training. I'm tellin' you I was sellin' thousands and thousands, but I had to come home.

LINDA. (*Crosses* R. *to him. He picks her up, hugs her.*) Oh, the whole block'll be at that game. Did you sell anything?

WILLY. (*Puts her down. Crosses* D. R.) I did five hundred gross in Providence and seven hundred gross in Boston.

LINDA. No! Wait a minute, I've got a pencil. (*Crosses after him. She pulls pencil and paper out of apron pocket.*) That makes your commission . . . (*Figures on his* L. *arm.*) Two hundred . . . My God! Two hundred and twelve dollars!

WILLY. (*Shaking her off arm.*) Well, I didn't figure it yet, but . . .

LINDA. (*Kindly.*) How much did you do?

WILLY. Well, I . . . I did . . . about a hundred and eighty gross in Providence. Well, no . . . it came to . . . roughly two hundred gross in the whole trip.

LINDA. (*Without hesitation.*) Two hundred gross . . . that's . . . (*She figures.*)

24

WILLY. (*Embattled, crosses to* C.) The trouble was that three of the stores were half closed for inventory in Boston. Otherwise I woulda broke records. . . .

LINDA. Well, it makes seventy dollars and some pennies. That's very good. (*Crosses* L. *to him.*)

WILLY. (*Blaming her.*) What do we owe?

LINDA. (*As* WILLY *crosses* L.) Well . . . on the first there's sixteen dollars on the refrigerator . . .

WILLY. Why sixteen? (*Turns.*)

LINDA. (*Apologizing.*) Well, the fan belt broke, so it was a dollar eighty.

WILLY. But it's brand-new.

LINDA. Well, the man said that's the way it is; till they work themselves in, y'know.

WILLY. (*Crossing* U. *into kitchen, goes* L. *of table.*) I hope we didn't get stuck on that machine.

LINDA. (*Crossing* U. *to* R. *of table.*) They got the biggest ads of any of them.

WILLY. I know, it's a fine machine. What else? (*Crosses* D. *out of kitchen.*)

LINDA. (*Crossing to below chair* R. *of table.*) Well . . . there's nine-sixty for the washing machine; then the roof, you got twenty-one dollars remaining. . . .

WILLY. It don't leak, does it?

LINDA. (*Still figuring on pad.*) No, they did a wonderful job. Then you owe Frank for the carburetor.

WILLY. (*Crossing* R. *to* C. *just past* LINDA.) I'm not going to pay that man! That goddam Chevrolet, they ought to prohibit the manufacture of that car!

LINDA. (*Not sad.*) Well, you owe him three and a half. (*Crossing to behind* WILLY, *staying in kitchen.*) And odds and ends, comes to around a hundred and twenty dollars by the fifteenth. (*Hugs him.*)

WILLY. A hundred and twenty dollars! My God, if business don't pick up I don't know what I'm gonna do.

LINDA. Well, next week you'll do better.

WILLY. Oh, I'll knock 'em dead next week. I'll go to Hartford. I'm very well liked in Hartford. You know the trouble is, Linda . . . People don't seem to take to me.

LINDA. Oh, don't be foolish.

WILLY. I know it when I walk in. They seem to laugh at me.

LINDA. (*Crossing* U. *to refrigerator, puts pad and pencil in apron pocket, gets stockings from sewing basket.*) Why? Why would they laugh at you? Don't talk that way, Willy.

WILLY. (*Crosses* D. R.) I don't know the reason for it, but they just pass me by. I'm not noticed.

LINDA. (*Looking at stockings. Cheerfully.*) But you're doin' wonderful, dear. You're making seventy to a hundred dollars a week.

WILLY. (*Talking more to himself than to her.*) But I gotta be at it ten, twelve hours a day. Other men . . . I don't know . . . they do it easier. I don't know why . . . I can't stop myself. . . . I talk too much. A man oughta come in with a few words. One thing about Charley. He's a man of few words, and they respect him.

LINDA. You don't talk too much, you're just lively. . . .

WILLY. (*To her. Smiles.*) Well, I figure, what the hell, life is short, a couple of jokes. (*To himself.*) I joke too much! (*The smile goes.*)

LINDA. Why? You're . . .

WILLY. (*Facing front, talking to himself.*) I'm fat. I'm very . . . foolish to look at, Linda. I didn't tell you, but Christmas time, I happened to be calling on F. H. Stewart's, and a salesman I know . . . as I was going in to see the buyer I heard him say something about . . . walrus. And I . . . I cracked him right across the face. I won't take that. I simply will not take that. But they do laugh at me . . . I know that. . . .

LINDA. Darling . . .

WILLY. I gotta overcome it. I know I gotta overcome it. I'm not dressing to advantage, maybe . . .

LINDA. (*Crossing* D., *bringing stockings and sewing basket, sits* L. *of table.*) Willy, darling. . . . You're the handsomest man in the world. (*Laughs lightly.* WOMAN *laughs as she enters* L., *behind and to* R. *of clothes hook as indicated on stage plan. Crosses* D. *to* R. *of second portal toward kitchen door. Takes jacket and hat from hook on portal and puts them on.* WOMAN *invisible to* LINDA.)

WILLY. Ah, no, Linda.

LINDA. To me you are. (*Slight pause.*) The handsomest. (*MUSIC CUE NO. 5.* LINDA *and* WOMAN *laugh together again.*) And the boys, Willy, few men are idolized by their children the way you are. . . . (*Puts on glasses. Mends stockings.*)

26

WILLY. (*With great feeling. Crosses* L. *slowly, straight across stage.*) You're the best there is, Linda, you're a pal, you know that? On the road . . . on the road I want to grab you sometimes and just kiss the life outa you. . . . (WOMAN *crosses to* D. L. *The laughter is loud and* WILLY *moves into a brightening area where* WOMAN *is standing, putting on her scarf, looking front and laughing softly. Crossing slowly to her.*) 'Cause I get so lonely . . . especially when business is bad and there's nobody to talk to. I get the feeling that I'll never sell anything again, that I won't make a living for you, or a business, a business for the boys. (WOMAN *is primping, looking front.*) There's so much I want to make for . . .

WOMAN. Me? You didn't make me, Willy. I picked you.

WILLY. (*Hugs her. Pleased.*) You picked me?

WOMAN. (*She is quite proper, his age.*) I did. I've been sitting at that desk watching all the salesmen go by, day in and day out. But you've got such a sense of humor, and I think you're a wonderful man.

WILLY. (*Behind her.*) Sure, sure. . . . (*His arms encircle her waist. Hugs her savagely.*) Why do you have to go now?

WOMAN. It's two o'clock. . . .

WILLY. No, come on in! (*He pulls on her, moving* U. S. *few steps.*)

WOMAN. My sisters'll be scandalized. . . . When'll you be back?

WILLY. Oh, two weeks about. Will you come up again?

WOMAN. (*Turns in his arms.*) Sure thing. You do make me laugh. It's good for me. (*Kisses him.*)

WILLY. (*Holding her at arm's length.*) You picked me, heh?

WOMAN. Sure. Because you're so sweet. And such a kidder.

WILLY. (*Crossing* U. *to trellis entrance.*) Well . . . I'll see you next time I'm in Boston.

WOMAN. I'll put you right through to the buyers.

WILLY. Right. Well . . . bottoms up! (*Slaps her on rear.*)

WOMAN. You just kill me, Willy. . . . You kill me. And thanks for the stockings. I love a lot of stockings. Well—good night.

WILLY. Good night. And keep your pores open!

WOMAN. Oh, Willy! (*Music fades out.* WOMAN *bursts out laughing and* LINDA'S *laughter blends in.* WOMAN *disappears into dark. And now from the brightening area at kitchen table.*)

LINDA. (WILLY *turns and goes to her.*) You are, Willy. The hand-

27

somest man. You've got no reason to feel that . . . (WILLY *puts hand gently over her mouth.*)

WILLY. (*To* LINDA, *who is sitting where she was at kitchen table, now darning pair of her silk stockings.*) I'll make it all up to you, Linda, I'll . . .

LINDA. (WILLY *puts arm around her, takes her* L. *hand, which has stocking on it.*) There's nothing to make up, dear, you're doing fine, better than . . .

WILLY. (*Of her mending.*) What's that?

LINDA. Just mending my stocking, they're so expensive . . .

WILLY. (*Furious.*) I won't have you mending stockings in this house! Now throw them out! (*She puts them in her pocket.* BERNARD *enters running from* D. L.)

BERNARD. (*Crossing to below porch. Great concern.*) Where is he? If he doesn't study . . . !

WILLY. (*Crossing to* BERNARD. *With great agitation.*) You'll give him the answers!

BERNARD. I do, but I can't on a Regents; that's a State exam! They're liable to arrest me! (LINDA *takes off glasses.*)

WILLY. (*To* LINDA.) Where is he? I'll whip him, I'll whip him!

LINDA. (*Crossing* D. *to* WILLY'S R., *carrying sewing basket.*) And he'd better give back that football, Willy, it's not nice . . .

WILLY. (*To* BERNARD.) Biff! Where is he? (*To* LINDA.) Why is he taking everything? . . .

LINDA. He's too rough with the girls, Willy, all the mothers are afraid of him!

WILLY. I'll whip him . . . !

BERNARD. He's·driving the car without a license! (WOMAN *heard laughing* L.)

WILLY. Shut up!

LINDA. All the mothers . . .

WILLY. Shut up!

BERNARD. (*Backing quietly away and out.*) Mr. Birnbaum says he's stuck up . . .

WILLY. Get outa here!

BERNARD. If he doesn't buckle down he'll flunk Math! (*He is gone off* L.)

LINDA. He's right, Willy, you've gotta . . .

WILLY. (*Explodes at her.*) There's nothing the matter with him! (*She is almost in tears and exits to bathroom. He follows her up to door to bedroom.*) You want him to be a worm like Bernard? He's got spirit, personality. . . . (*Turns to above table. He is all alone, wilting and staring.*) Loaded with it. Loaded! . . . What is he stealing? He's giving it back, isn't he? (HAPPY, *having waked up and got out of bed, is coming downstairs in his pajamas.*) Why is he stealing? What did I tell him? (*To* HAPPY, *on steps.*) I never in my life told him anything but decent things. Why is he . . . (*Suddenly realizes he is talking to* HAPPY.)

HAPPY. (*Crosses to* WILLY.) Let's go now, come on.

WILLY. (*Crosses, sits* L. *of table.*) Huh! Why did she have to wax the floors herself? Every time she waxes the floors she keels over. She knows that!

HAPPY. (*Sits on table, above* WILLY.) Sshh—take it easy. What brought you back tonight?

WILLY. I got an awful scare; nearly hit a kid in Yonkers. God!— Why didn't I go to Alaska with my brother Ben that time? Ben!— that man was a genius, that man was success incarnate! What a mistake; he begged me to go. . . .

HAPPY. Well, there's no use in . . .

WILLY. You guys. . . . There was a man started with the clothes on his back and ended up with diamond mines!

HAPPY. Boy, some day I'd like to know how he did it!

WILLY. What's the mystery? The man knew what he wanted and went out and got it! Walked into a jungle, and comes out, the age of twenty-one, and he's rich! The world is an oyster, but you don't crack it open on a mattress!

HAPPY. Pop, I told you I'm gonna retire you for life.

WILLY. You'll retire me for life on your seventy goddam dollars a week? And your women and your car and your apartment and you'll retire me for life! (CHARLEY *appears in door from* U. L.) Christ's sake, I couldn't get past Yonkers today! Where are you guys, where are you? The woods are burning! I can't drive a car! (CHARLEY *is a large man, slow of speech, laconic, immovable. In all he says, despite what he says, there is pity, and now, trepidation. He has a robe over pajamas, slippers on his feet.*)

CHARLEY. Everything all right?

HAPPY. Yeah, Charley, everything's . . .

WILLY. What's the matter?

CHARLEY. (*Crosses in a step, closes kitchen door.*) I heard some

29

noise, I thought something happened. Can't we do something about the walls? You sneeze in here and in my house hats blow off.

HAPPY. (*Rises.*) Let's go to bed, Dad, come on. . . . (CHARLEY *signals* HAPPY *to go.*)

WILLY. (*Rises, crosses below to* R.) You go ahead, I'm not tired at the moment. (CHARLEY *indicates to* HAPPY *that he'll take care of* WILLY.)

HAPPY. (*To* WILLY.) Take it easy, huh?

WILLY. (*Grunts.*) Yeah! (HAPPY *exits upstairs.*) What're you doin' up?

CHARLEY. (*Crossing to chair* L. *of table.*) Couldn't sleep good. I had a heartburn.

WILLY. Well, you don't know how to eat.

CHARLEY. I eat with my mouth.

WILLY. No, you're ignorant. You gotta know about vitamins and things like that.

CHARLEY. (*Sits chair* L. *of table.*) Come on, let's shoot? Tire you out a little.

WILLY. (*Hesitates.*) All right, you got cards? (*Sits* R. *of table.*)

CHARLEY. (*Taking cards from his pocket.*) Yeah, I got them. Some place. What is it with those vitamins? (*Trying to take* WILLY'S *mind off his trouble.*)

WILLY. They build up your bones. Chemistry.

CHARLEY. Yeah, but there's no bones in a heartburn. (*Deals cards. Four cards to* WILLY, *four to himself, four face up on table.*)

WILLY. What are you talkin' about? Do you know the first thing about it?

CHARLEY. Don't get insulted.

WILLY. Don't talk about something you don't know anything about. (*They are ready to play. Pause.*)

CHARLEY. What're you doin' home?

WILLY. A little trouble with the car. (*Throws one card.*)

CHARLEY. Oh. (*Pause.*) I'd like to take a trip to California. (*Takes a trick.*)

WILLY. Don't say. (*Throws one card.*)

CHARLEY. (*Bends forward, fussing with cards on table.*) You want a job? (*Looks up at him.*)

WILLY. I got a job, I told you that. (*Looks suspiciously at* CHARLEY. *Slight pause.*) What the hell are you offering me a job for?

CHARLEY. Don't get insulted.

WILLY. Don't insult me.

CHARLEY. I don't see no sense in it. (*Throws one card.*) You don't have to go on this way.

WILLY. (*Strong.*) I got a good job. (*Slight pause.*) What do you keep comin' in here for?

CHARLEY. You want me to go? (*Throws cards down—starts up.*)

WILLY. (*Leans across table, grabs* CHARLEY'S *arm. Pause. Withering.*) Charley, I can't understand it. He's going back to Texas again. What the hell is that?

CHARLEY. Let him go.

WILLY. I got nothin' to give him, Charley, I'm clean, I'm clean.

CHARLEY. He won't starve. None a them starve. Forget about him.

WILLY. Then what have I got to remember?

CHARLEY. You take it too hard. To hell with it. When a deposit bottle is broken you don't get your nickel back.

WILLY. That's easy enough for you to say.

CHARLEY. That ain't easy for me to say. (*They pick up cards.*)

WILLY. (*Takes three-card trick.*) Did you see the ceiling I put up in the living room?

CHARLEY. Yeah, that's a piece of work. (*Throws one card.*) To put up a ceiling is a mystery to me. How do you do it?

WILLY. What's the difference? (*Takes a trick.*)

CHARLEY. Well, talk about it.

WILLY. (*Irritated.*) You gonna put up a ceiling?

CHARLEY. How could I put up a ceiling? (*Throws last card, deals: four to* WILLY, *four to himself.*)

WILLY. (*Shouting.*) Then what the hell are you bothering me for?

CHARLEY. You're insulted again.

WILLY. A man who can't handle tools is not a man. You're disgusting.

CHARLEY. (*Hurt.*) Don't call me disgusting, Willy. (*Slams pack* D. *after completing deal.*)

WILLY. I'm getting awfully tired, Ben. (BEN'S *MUSIC CUE NO. 6 is heard.*)

CHARLEY. (*Picks up cards.*) Good, keep playing; you'll sleep better. . . . Did you call me Ben? (UNCLE BEN *enters, a stolid man, in his sixties, with a moustache and an authoritative air. He is utterly certain of his destiny, and there is the aura of far places about him. He enters carrying umbrella and valise and smoking cigarette in holder, and looks around at the place like a stranger.*

BEN *puts valise by trellis,* R., *crosses* D. *looking at balcony, at imaginary clock, then at his watch.*)

WILLY. That's funny. For a second there you reminded me of my brother Ben.

BEN. I only have a few minutes. (*Strolls* D. R., *inspecting the place.* CHARLEY *and* WILLY *continue playing.*)

CHARLEY. You never heard from him again, heh? Since that time?

WILLY. Didn't Linda tell you? Couple of weeks ago we got a letter from his wife in Africa. He died.

CHARLEY. That's so.

BEN. (*Chuckling.*) So this is Brooklyn, eh? (*Moves up and* L. *to* C. *of* R. *of position of kitchen, looking around. Stamps out cigarette.*)

CHARLEY. Maybe you're in for some of his money?

WILLY. Naa, he had seven sons. There's just one opportunity I had with that man. . . . (*Throws a card.*)

BEN. I must make a train, William; there are several properties I'm looking at in Alaska. (CHARLEY *takes a trick.*)

WILLY. Sure, sure! . . . If I'd've gone with him to Alaska that time . . . everything would've been totally different. (*Takes a trick.*)

CHARLEY. Go on, you'd froze to death up there.

WILLY. What're you talking about . . . ?

BEN. Opportunity is tremendous in Alaska, William. Surprised you're not up there. (*Crosses* D.)

WILLY. Sure, tremendous. (CHARLEY *throws a card.*)

CHARLEY. Heh?

WILLY. There was the only man I ever met who knew the answers.

CHARLEY. Who?

BEN. How are you all? (WILLY *takes three-card trick.*)

WILLY. (*Taking a pot, smiling.*) Fine, fine.

CHARLEY. (*Indicating cards.*) Pretty sharp tonight.

BEN. Is Mother living with you?

WILLY. No, she died a long time ago.

CHARLEY. Who?

BEN. (*Crossing* U. *to* C. *of* R. *kitchen position.*) That's too bad. Fine specimen of a lady, Mother.

WILLY. (*To* CHARLEY.) Heh?

BEN. I'd hoped to see the old girl.

CHARLEY. Who died?

BEN. Heard anything from Father, have you?

WILLY. (*Unnerved.*) What do you mean, who died?

CHARLEY. What're you talkin' about? (*Throws a card. Starts to take trick.*)

BEN. (*Looking at watch.*) William, it's half-past eight!

WILLY. (*As though to dispel his confusion, angrily stops* CHARLEY's *hand.*) That's my build!

CHARLEY. I put the ace . . .

WILLY. (*Rises.*) If you don't know how to play the game I'm not gonna throw my money away on you!

CHARLEY. It was my ace, for God's sake! (*Gathers cards together.*)

WILLY. (*Crossing* U. *above table.*) I'm through, I'm through!

BEN. When did Mother die? (*Crosses* D.)

WILLY. (*Crosses above to door. To* BEN.) Long ago. . . . (*To* CHARLEY.) Since the beginning you never knew how to play cards.

CHARLEY. (*Picks up cards and goes toward door.*) All right! Next time I'll bring a deck with five aces.

WILLY. I don't play that kind of game!

CHARLEY. (*Turning to him.*) You ought to be ashamed of yourself!

WILLY. Yeah?

CHARLEY. Yeah! (*Goes out* U. L. *kitchen door. Music fades out.*)

WILLY. Ignoramus! (*Leaves kitchen after* CHARLEY *goes out, slams kitchen door. Goes to* BEN, R. C. *on apron below kitchen. Puts hands on* BEN'S *arms, shakes him.*) Ben! I've been waiting for you for so long! What's the answer? How did you do it?

BEN. Oh, there's a story in that. (LINDA *enters from* U. L. *behind house, carrying wash basket. Crosses* D. *on to apron.*)

LINDA. Is this Ben? (*Puts basket down.*)

BEN. (*Crossing* L. *to her. Takes off hat. Gallantly.*) How do you do, my dear. (*She wipes hands on apron, then shakes hands.*)

LINDA. (*As* WILLY *crosses to* BEN.) Where've you been all these years? Willy's always wondered why you . . .

WILLY. (*Pulling* BEN *away from her impatiently. Taking him* D. R.) Where is Dad? Didn't you follow him? How did you get started?

BEN. Well, I don't know how much you remember . . .

WILLY. Well, when you left I was just a baby, of course, only

33

three or four years old. . . . (LINDA *picks up basket, crossing slowly to* C.)

BEN. Three years and eleven months.

WILLY. What a memory, Ben!

BEN. (*Putting hat on.*) I have many enterprises, William, and I have never kept books.

WILLY. I remember I was sitting under the wagon in . . . was it Nebraska?

BEN. It was South Dakota, and I gave you a bunch of wild flowers. . . .

WILLY. Sure, the flowers. I remember you walking away down some open road. . . .

BEN. (*Laughs.*) I was going to find Father in Alaska.

WILLY. Where is he?

BEN. At that age I had a very faulty view of geography, William. I discovered after a few days that I was heading due south, so instead of Alaska I ended up in Africa. (*Turns* L. *to* LINDA.)

LINDA. (*Back up a step.*) Africa!

WILLY. The Gold Coast!

BEN. Principally diamond mines.

LINDA. (*Back up a step.*) Diamond mines!

BEN. Yes, my dear. But I've only a few minutes . . .

WILLY. No. . . . Boys! Boys!! (*Boys:* U. R. *behind house, calling* "*Hup, Hup!*" *Young* BIFF *and* HAPPY *appear, running from behind house,* U. R. WILLY *is between boys and* BEN.) Listen to this. This is your Uncle Ben, a great man! . . . Tell my boys, Ben! (HAPPY *flops on stomach,* D. R., BIFF *kneels above him.*)

BEN. Why, boys . . . when I was seventeen I walked into the jungle, and when I was twenty-one I walked out. . . . (*He laughs.*) And by God I was rich! (*Walks* L. *to* C. LINDA *backs up.*)

WILLY. (*To boys.*) You see what I been talking about? The greatest things can happen!

BEN. (*Crosses* R. *to* WILLY, *glancing at his watch.*) I have an appointment in Ketchikan Tuesday week.

WILLY. (*Stops him.*) No, Ben, please. . . . Tell about Dad. (*To boys.*) I want my boys to hear. I want them to know the kind of stock they spring from. All I remember is a man with a big beard . . . and I was in Mamma's lap . . . sitting around a fire . . . and some kind of high music. (*MUSIC CUE NO. 7.*)

BEN. His flute. He played the flute. . . .

34

WILLY. Sure, the flute, that's right!

BEN. (*Boasting.*) Father was a very great, and a very wild-hearted man. (BIFF *rises slowly, crosses below* WILLY *to* BEN.) We would start in Boston, and he'd toss the whole family into the wagon, and then he'd drive the team right across the country; through Ohio, and Indiana, Michigan, Illinois and all the western states. And we'd stop in the towns and sell the flutes that he'd made on the way. Great inventor, Father. With one gadget he made more in a week than a man like you could make in a lifetime. (*Crosses* L. *to* L. C. *Music fades out.*)

WILLY. (*Shoving* BIFF *toward* BEN.) That's just the way I'm bringing them up, Ben. . . . Rugged, well-liked, all around . . .

BEN. ·Yeah? Well, (*To* BIFF.) hit that, boy . . . hard as you can. (*He pounds his stomach.*)

BIFF. Oh, no, sir. . . .

BEN. (*Takes a boxing stance.*) Come on, get to me! (*Laughs.*)

WILLY. Go to it, Biff; go ahead, show him!

BIFF. Okay! (*He cocks his fists and starts in.*)

LINDA. (*To* WILLY.) Why must he fight, dear? (*Puts basket* D. *up by porch steps near door to kitchen.*)

BEN. (*Sparring with him.*) Good boy! Good boy!

WILLY. How's that, Ben, heh?

HAPPY. Give him the left, Biff!

LINDA. Why are you fighting?

BEN. Good boy! (*Suddenly comes in, trips* BIFF, *who rolls* D. L. *and stands over him, the point of his umbrella poised over* BIFF'S *eye.*)

LINDA. (*Crossing to above and* L. *of* BIFF.) Look out, Biff!

BIFF. (*On his back.*) Gee!

BEN. (*Patting his knee.*) Never fight fair with a stranger, boy . . . you'll never get out of the jungle that way. (*Without pause, takes off hat, takes* LINDA'S *hand and bows.*) It was an honor and a pleasure to meet you, Linda. (*She withdraws her hand coldly.*)

LINDA. (*Frightened.*) Have a nice . . . trip. (*Crosses* U., *picks up wash.*)

BEN. (*Crossing* R. *to* WILLY.) And good luck to your . . . What do you do?

WILLY. (*Feeling inferior.*) Selling. . . .

BEN. (*Puts hat on.*) Yes. Well . . . (*Crosses above* WILLY.)

WILLY. (*Stops* BEN.) No, Ben, I don't want you to think . . .

35

(*Takes* BEN'S *arm to show him.*) It's Brooklyn, I know, but we hunt, too. . . .

BEN. (*At* R. *of* WILLY.) Really now.

WILLY. (*Naively.*) Oh, sure, there's snakes and rabbits and . . . that's why I moved out here. . . . Why, Biff can fell any one of these trees in no time! Boys!—go right over to where they're building the apartment house and get some sand; we're gonna rebuild the entire front stoop right now! Watch this, Ben!

BIFF. Yes, sir! (*Crosses. Runs* U. L. *behind house.*) On the double, Hap!

HAPPY. (*As both run off* U. L. *behind house.*) I lost weight, Pop, you notice? (CHARLEY *enters in knickers, sweater and cap from* U. L. *even before boys are gone.*)

CHARLEY. (*Crossing to* C. *to* L. *of* WILLY.) Listen, if they steal any more from that building the watchman'll put the cops on them!

LINDA. (*Crosses to* L. *of* CHARLEY. *To* WILLY.) Don't let Biff . . . (BEN *laughs lustily.*)

WILLY. (*Taking* BEN, *crossing* D. R.) You shoulda seen the lumber they brought home last week. (BEN *is laughing.*) At least a dozen six-by-tens worth all kindsa money. . . .

CHARLEY. Listen, if that watchman . . .

WILLY. I gave them hell, you understand . . . but I got a couple of fearless characters there. . . .

CHARLEY. Willy, the jails are full of fearless characters.

BEN. And the stock exchange, friend!

WILLY. (*Laughing, with* BEN.) Where are the rest of your pants?

CHARLEY. My wife bought them.

WILLY. Now all you need is a golf club and you can go upstairs and go to sleep. (*To* BEN.) Great athlete! Between him and his son Bernard they can't hammer a nail!

CHARLEY. How did you do in Portland this trip?

WILLY. Decapitated them. Ben, I can't handle the volume.

LINDA. He'd've done better if they hadn't been closed for inventory.

WILLY. I had the greatest week in my history.

BERNARD. (*Rushing in from* U. L.) The watchman's chasing Biff!

WILLY. (*Crosses* L. *a few steps. Angrily.*) Shut up! He's not stealing anything!

LINDA. (*Hurries off toward* U. L., *alarmed.*) Where is he? Biff, dear! (*She exits* U. L., *behind house.* CHARLEY *crosses to* D. L.)

WILLY. (*Crosses to* C.) There's nothing wrong, what's the matter with you?

BEN. Nervy boy, good!

WILLY. (*Laughing, turning to* BEN.) Oh, nerves of iron, that Biff. . . .

CHARLEY. Don't know how you do the business, Willy. All the salesmen in the city are coming back bleeding from New England, can't sell a nickel for three cents and you're doin' great, heh?

WILLY. (*Crossing to* D. L.) It's contacts, Charley, I got important contacts!

CHARLEY. Glad to hear it, Willy. Come in later, we'll shoot a little casino—I'll take some of your Portland money. (*Laughs at* WILLY, *exits* U. L.)

WILLY. (*Turning to* BEN.) Business is bad, but not for me, of course. (*MUSIC CUE NO. 8.*)

BEN. (*Crosses* U.) I'll stop by on my way back to Africa.

WILLY. (D. L.) Can't you stay a few days? You're just what I need, Ben, because I . . . I have a fine position here, but I . . . well, Dad left when I was such a baby and I never had a chance to talk to him and I still feel . . . kind of temporary about myself.

BEN. (*Getting valise.*) I'll be late for the train.

WILLY. Ben, my boys . . . can't we talk?—they'd go into the jaws of hell for me, see, but I . . .

BEN. William, you're being first-rate with your boys. Outstanding, manly chaps!

WILLY. (*Hanging on to his words.*) Oh, Ben, that's good to hear! Because sometimes I'm afraid that I'm not teaching them the right kind of . . . (BEN *crosses* U. *to trellis.* WILLY *speaks anxiously.*) Ben, how should I teach them?

BEN. (*With great weight to each word, and a certain vicious audacity.*) William, when I walked into the jungle, I was seventeen. When I walked out I was twenty-one . . . and by God, I was rich! (*Goes away* U. R. LINDA *enters from bathroom with* WILLY'S *coat, thread and needle. Puts coat on chair* L. *of kitchen table, then crosses out through kitchen door to* WILLY *at* C. *stage.*)

WILLY. . . . Was rich! That's just the spirit I want to imbue them with! To walk into a jungle! I was right! I was right! I was right!

37

(BEN *is gone, and* WILLY *is still speaking to him.* LINDA, *in night-gown and robe comes down to his* L. *He looks at her. Music fades out.*)

LINDA. Willy, dear? Willy?

WILLY. I was right! (*Turns his head.*)

LINDA. Did you have some cheese? (*He can't answer.*) It's very late, darling. (*Taking him* L.) Come to bed, heh?

WILLY. (*Looks straight up. Crosses* L. *past her.*) Gotta break your neck to see a star in this yard.

LINDA. You coming in?

WILLY. Whatever happened to that diamond watch-fob? Remember?—when Ben came from Africa that time? Didn't he give me a watch fob with a diamond in it?

LINDA. You pawned it, dear—twelve, thirteen years ago—for Biff's radio correspondence course. (BIFF, *in pajamas, gets out of bed, starts* D. *stairs.* HAPPY, *in pajamas, gets out of bed, crosses* L., *lights cigarette.*)

WILLY. Gee, that was a beautiful thing. I'll take a walk.

LINDA. But you're in your slippers.

WILLY. I was right! I was! (*He starts out. Half to her, as he goes, shaking his head.*) What a man! There was a man worth talking to. . . .

LINDA. (*Calling.*) But in your slippers, Willy. . .

WILLY. (*Off* U. L. *Shouting.*) I was right. (*He is gone* U. L. LINDA *crosses back into kitchen, closing door.*)

BIFF. (*At bottom of stairs.*) What is he doing out there? (HAPPY *comes downstairs.*)

LINDA. (*Crosses, picks up coat.*) Ssh!

BIFF. (*Following after her.*) God Almighty, Mom, how long has he been doing this?

LINDA. (*Sits chair* L. *of table.*) Don't, he'll hear you.

BIFF. (*Crosses above chair* R. *of table.*) What the hell is the matter with him?!

LINDA. (*Puts on glasses. Irritated at his tone.*) It'll pass by morning.

BIFF. Shouldn't we do anything?

LINDA. (*Sewing lining of coat.*) Oh, my dear, you should do a lot of things, but there's nothing to do, so go to sleep.

HAPPY. (*Crossing* L. *to refrigerator.*) I never heard him so loud, Mom.

LINDA. Well, come around more often, you'll hear him.

BIFF. Why didn't you ever write me about this, Mom?

LINDA. How could I write to you? For over three months you had no address.

BIFF. (*Leaning across table on coat.*) I was on the move. . . . But you know I thought of you all the time. You know that, don't you, pal?

LINDA. (*Takes his hands off coat.*) I know, dear, I know. (*Sews.*) But he likes to have a letter . . . just to know that there's still a possibility for better things.

BIFF. (*To* HAPPY.) He's not like this all the time, is he? (HAPPY *nods.*)

LINDA. It's when you come home he's always the worst.

BIFF. When I come home?

LINDA. When you write you're coming he's all smiles, and talks about the future, and . . . he's just wonderful. And then the closer you seem to come the more shaky he gets, and then . . . by the time you get here . . . he's arguing, and he seems angry at you. I think it's just that maybe he can't bring himself to . . . to open up to you. Why are you so hateful to each other? Why is that?

BIFF. (*Evasively.*) I'm not hateful, Mom. . . .

LINDA. But you no sooner come in the door than you're fighting!

BIFF. (*Appealing to her.*) I don't know why. I mean to change. . . . I'm tryin', Mom, you understand?

LINDA. (*Stops sewing.*) Are you home to stay now?

BIFF. (*Crosses* R.) I don't know. I want to look around, see what's doin'. . . .

LINDA. Biff, you can't look around all your life, can you?

BIFF. (*Crosses* L. *to above her. Leans on table.*) I just can't take hold, Mom. I can't take hold of some kind of a life.

LINDA. Biff, a man is not a bird, to come and go with the springtime. . . .

BIFF. Your hair . . . (*Touches her hair.*) Your hair got so gray.

LINDA. (*Pushes his hand away, starts sewing.*) Oh, it's been gray since you were in high school. I just stopped dyeing it, that's all.

BIFF. (*Trying to cheer her up.*) Dye it again, will ya? (*Crossing, sits* R. *of table.*) I don't want my pal looking old. (*Smiling.*)

LINDA. You're such a boy! You think you can go away for a year

39

and . . . You've got to get it into your head now that one day you'll knock on this door and there'll be strange people here. . . .

BIFF. What are you talking about? You're not even sixty, Mom.

LINDA. But what about your father?

BIFF. (*Lamely.*) Well, I meant him, too.

HAPPY. He admires Pop. . . .

LINDA. Biff, if you don't have any feeling for him then you can't have any feeling for me.

BIFF. (*Leans forward on coat.*) Sure I can, Mom.

LINDA. (*Rises, picks up finished coat. Speaks louder.*) No: You can't just come to see me, because I love him. (*Now, with a threat, but only a threat, of tears.*) He's the dearest man in the world to me, and I won't have anyone making him feel unwanted, and low and blue. (*Crosses slowly to chair over R., and tenderly hangs coat over back of it.*) You've got to make up your mind now, there's no leeway any more—either he's your father and you pay him that respect or else you're not to come here. I know he's not easy to get along with—nobody knows that better than me—but ——

WILLY. (*From up L., with a laugh.*) Hey, hey, Biffo!

BIFF. (*Starts to go out.*) What the hell is the matter with him!

LINDA. (*Grabs BIFF'S L. arm.*) Don't . . . don't go near him!

BIFF. Stop making excuses for him! He always, always wiped the floor with you. Never had an ounce of respect for you.

HAPPY. (*Crossing R. to BIFF.*) He's always had respect for . . .

BIFF. What the hell do you know about it? (LINDA *crosses .R., smooths coat.*)

HAPPY. Just don't call him crazy!

BIFF. He's got no character. (*Breaks off.*) Charley wouldn't do this—spewing out that vomit from his mind.

HAPPY. Charley never had to cope with what he's got to. . . .

BIFF. (*Above table.*) People are worse off than Willy Loman; believe me, I've seen them!

LINDA. (*Crossing to BIFF.*) Then make Charley your father, Biff. You can't do that, can you? (BIFF *slowly sits chair L. of table.*) I don't say he's a great man. Willy Loman never made a lot of money; his name was never in the paper; he's not the finest character that ever lived. But he's a human being, and a terrible thing is happening to him. So attention must be paid. He's not to be allowed to fall into his grave like an old dog. *Attention, atten-*

tion must be finally paid to such a person. You called him crazy
. . . (*Turns away* R., *takes off glasses.*)
BIFF. I didn't mean . . .
LINDA. (*Turns back again, puts glasses in pocket.*) No, a lot of
people think he's lost his . . . balance. (*Pause, then with re-
proach.*) But you don't have to be very smart to know what his
trouble is. The man is exhausted.
HAPPY. Sure! (*Crosses* L.)
LINDA. (*Crossing* R. *to chair over* R., *straightens coat on chair.*)
A small man can be just as exhausted as a great man. He works
for a company thirty-six years this March, opens up unheard-of
territories to their trademark, and now in his old age they take
his salary away. . . .
HAPPY. (*Rises. Indignantly.*) I didn't know that, Mom!
LINDA. You never asked, my dear! Now that you get your spending
money some place else you don't trouble your mind with him.
HAPPY. But I gave you money last . . .
LINDA. (*Thrown away.*) Christmas time, fifty dollars! To fix the
hot water, it cost ninety-seven fifty! (*Crosses* U. *to above table.*)
For *five weeks* he's been on *straight commission*, like a beginner,
an unknown. . . .
BIFF. Those ungrateful bastards . . . !
LINDA. Are they any worse than his sons? When he brought them
business when he was young, they were glad to see him. But now
his old—(*Crosses* R., *smooths coat on chair over* R.) friends, the
old buyers that loved him so and always found some order to
hand him in a pinch—they're all dead, retired. He used to be able
to make six, seven calls a day in Boston. Now he takes his valises
out of the car and puts them back and takes them out again and
he's exhausted. Instead of walking he talks now. He drives seven
hundred miles and when he gets there no one knows him any
more, no one welcomes him. (*Crosses to* U. R. *corner of table.*)
And what goes through a man's mind, driving seven hundred
miles home without having earned a cent? Why shouldn't he talk
to himself? Why?—When he has to go to Charley and borrow
fifty dollars a week and pretend to me that it's his pay?
HAPPY. (*Pained.*) God!
LINDA. (*Crosses* R., *sits chair over* R.) How long can that go on?
How long? You see what I'm sitting here and waiting for? And
you tell me he has no character? The man who never worked a

41

day but for your benefit? When does he get the medal for that? Is this his reward—to turn around at the age of sixty-three and find his sons, who he loved better than his life, one a philandering bum ——

HAPPY. Mom!

LINDA. That's all you are, my baby! (*To* BIFF. *Quiet, intense.*) And you! What happened to the love you had for him? (*Leaning forward, grasping back of chair* R. *of table.*) You were such pals. . . . How you used to talk to him on the phone every night! How lonely he was till he could come home to you! (*Short pause.*)

BIFF. (*Rises, crosses* R. *to above* LINDA. *Forcing himself.*) All right, Mom. I'll live here in my room, and I'll get a job. . . . I'll keep away from him, that's all.

LINDA. No, Biff . . . you can't stay here and fight all the time.

BIFF. He threw me out of this house, remember that.

LINDA. Why did he do that? I never knew *why*?

BIFF. Because I know he's a fake and he doesn't like anybody around who knows!

LINDA. Why a fake? In what way? What do you mean?

BIFF. (*Crossing* L. *to* L. *of table. Holding in his anger.*) Just don't lay it all at my feet. It's between me and him; that's all I have to say. I'll chip in from now on. He'll settle for half my pay check—he'll be all right. I'm going to bed. (*He starts* R. HAPPY *puts cigarette out in ashtray on top of refrigerator.*)

LINDA. (*Quietly.*) He won't be all right.

BIFF. (*Agitated, crosses* L. *to* L. *of table, furious.*) I hate this city and I'll stay here. . . . Now what do you want?

LINDA. (*Simply.*) He's dying, Biff.

BIFF. (*Subdued.*) Why is he dying?

LINDA. He's been trying to kill himself.

BIFF. How?

LINDA. I live from day to day ——

BIFF. What're you talking about?

LINDA. Remember I wrote you that he smashed up the car again? In February?

BIFF. Well?

LINDA. The insurance inspector came. He said that they have evidence. That all these accidents in the last year . . . weren't . . . weren't . . . accidents.

HAPPY. (*Crossing* R. *to above table.*) How can they tell that? That's a lie.

LINDA. It seems there's a woman . . . (*Takes a breath as:*) And this woman . . .

BIFF. (*Crosses few steps* R. *Sharply, but contained.*) What woman?

LINDA. What?

BIFF. (*Back up few steps.*) Nothing. Go ahead.

LINDA. What did you say?

BIFF. Nothing. I just said what woman?

HAPPY. What about her?

LINDA. (*Factually.*) Well, it seems she was walking down the road and saw his car. (BIFF *crosses below table slowly, sits chair* R.) She says that he wasn't driving fast at all, and that he didn't skid. She says he came to that little bridge, and then deliberately smashed into the railing, and it was only the shallowness of the water that saved him.

BIFF. Oh, no, he probably just fell asleep again.

LINDA. I don't think he fell asleep.

BIFF. Why not?

LINDA. Last month . . . (*With great difficulty.*) Oh, boys, it's so hard to say a thing like this! He's just a big stupid man to you, but I tell you there's more good in him than in many other people. . . . I was looking for a fuse . . . the lights blew out and I went down the cellar . . . and behind the fuse box . . . it happened to fall out . . . was a length of rubber pipe . . . just short.

HAPPY. No kidding.

LINDA. There's a little attachment on the end of it. . . . I knew right away. And sure enough on the bottom of the water heater there's a new little nipple on the gas pipe.

HAPPY. (*Angered.*) That . . . jerk!

BIFF. Did you have it taken off?

LINDA. (*Slightly reprimanding him.*) I'm . . . I'm ashamed to. (*Sincerely—emotionless.*) How can I mention it to him? Every day I go down and take away that little rubber pipe. But . . . when he comes home . . . I put it back where it was. How can I insult him that way? I don't know what to do. I live from day to day, boys. I tell you, I know every thought in his mind. It sounds so old-fashioned and silly, but I tell you he put his whole life into you and you've turned your backs on him. Biff, I swear to God; Biff, his life is in your hands!

HAPPY. (*To* BIFF, *crosses* L. *few steps.*) How do you like that damned fool!

BIFF. (*Kneeling, kissing her cheek, then hugging her.*) All right, pal, all right. It's all settled now. I've been remiss. . . . I know that, Mom. But now I'll stay, and I swear to you, I'll apply myself. (*Kneeling in front of her, in a fever of self-reproach and striving, and a sense of loss.*) It's just . . . you see, Mom . . . I don't fit in business—not that I won't try, I'll try, and I'll make good. . . .

HAPPY. (*Crosses to above* BIFF.) Sure you will. The trouble with you in business was you never tried to please people.

BIFF. (*Over his* L. *shoulder.*) I know, I . . .

HAPPY. Like when you worked for Harrisons'. Bob Harrison said you were tops and then you go and do some damn fool thing like whistling whole songs in the elevator like a comedian.

BIFF. (*Rises, crosses below table around it to stove.*) So what? I like to whistle sometimes. . . .

HAPPY. (*Following* BIFF.) You don't raise a guy to a responsible job who whistles in the elevator.

LINDA. Well, don't argue about it now.

HAPPY. (*At* L. *of* BIFF.) Like when you'd go off and swim in the middle of the day instead of taking the line around . . .

BIFF. (*Resentment rising.*) Well, don't you run off? You take off sometimes, don't you? On a nice summer day . . . ?

HAPPY. Yeah, but I cover myself.

LINDA. Boys! (*Crosses* U. *to* BIFF.)

HAPPY. (*Crosses* U.) If I'm going to take a fade the boss can call any number where I'm supposed to be and they'll swear to him that I just left. I'll tell you something that I hate to say, Biff, but in the business world some of them think you're crazy.

BIFF. (*Angered.*) Screw the business world! (LINDA *crosses to* HAPPY. *Pushes him* L., *trying to cover his mouth with her hand.*)

HAPPY. All right, screw it, great, but cover yourself! (WILLY *appears in kitchen door from* U. L.)

LINDA. Hap, Hap!

BIFF. (*Crosses* D.) I don't care what you think! (*Crosses* U.) They've laughed at Dad for years, and you know why? (*Crosses* D.) Because we don't belong in this nuthouse of a city! (*Starts up, sees* WILLY.) We should be mixing cement on some open plain, or . . . or carpenters. A carpenter is allowed to whistle! (*Crosses to* D. R. *corner of kitchen.* LINDA *crosses* HAPPY *to above chair* L. *of table.* HAPPY *crosses two steps* R.)

WILLY. Even your grandfather was better than a carpenter. (*Pause. They watch him.*) You never grew up. Bernard does not whistle on the elevator, I assure you. (*Crosses in, closes door.*)

BIFF. (*As though to laugh him out of it.*) Yeah, but you do, Pop.

WILLY. I never in my life whistled on an elevator! And who in the business world thinks I'm crazy?

BIFF. I didn't mean it like that, Pop. Now don't make a whole thing out of it, will ya?

WILLY. Go back to the West! Be a carpenter, a cowboy, enjoy yourself!

LINDA. Willy, he was just saying . . .

WILLY. I heard what he said!

HAPPY. (*Trying to quiet him.*) Hey, Pop, come on now. . . .

WILLY. (*Continuing over* HAPPY's *line.*) They laugh at me, heh? Go to Filene's, go to the Hub, go to Slattery's, Boston. Call out the name Willy Loman and see what happens! Big shot!

BIFF. All right, Pop. . . .

WILLY. Big!

BIFF. (*Intense.*) All right!!! (LINDA *crosses to* BIFF, *seats him in chair over* R.)

WILLY. Why do you always insult me?

BIFF. I didn't say a word. (*To* LINDA.) Did I say a word?

LINDA. (*Arm around* BIFF.) He didn't say anything, Willy.

WILLY. (*Starting up.*) All right, good night, good night.

LINDA. (*Trying to get* BIFF *to talk.*) Willy, dear, he just decided . . .

WILLY. (*Stops. To* BIFF.) If you get tired hanging around tomorrow, paint the ceiling I put on in the living-room.

BIFF. (*Calm.*) I'm leaving early tomorrow.

HAPPY. He's going to see Bill Oliver, Pop.

WILLY. (*Interested.*) Oliver? For what?

BIFF. (*With reserve, but trying, trying.*) He always said he'd stake me. I'd like to go into business, so maybe I can take him up on it.

LINDA. Isn't that wonderful?

WILLY. (*Crosses* HAPPY *to above table.*) Don't interrupt. What's

45

wonderful about? There's fifty men in the city of New York who'd stake him. (*To* HAPPY.) Sporting goods?

BIFF. I guess so. I know something about it and . . .

WILLY. (*Crosses to* R. *of table.*) He knows something about it! You know sporting goods better than Spalding, for God's sake! How much is he giving you?

BIFF. I don't know, I didn't even see him yet, but . . .

WILLY. Then what're you talkin' about?

BIFF. (*Angering.*) Well, all I said was I'm gonna see him, that's all!

WILLY. Ah, you're counting your chickens again.

BIFF. (*Rises, starts* L. *below table for the out of kitchen door.*) Oh, Jesus, I'm going . . . !

WILLY. (*Calling after him.*) Don't curse in this house!

BIFF. (*Turning at* D. L. *of kitchen.*) Since when did you get so clean?

HAPPY. (*To stop it.*) Wait a . . .

WILLY. Don't use that language to me! I won't have it!

HAPPY. (*Shouts, grabs* BIFF.) Wait a minute! I got an idea. I got a feasible idea. Come here, Biff, let's talk this over now, let's talk some sense here. When I was down in Florida last time, I thought of a great idea to sell sporting goods. It just came back to me. You and I, Biff . . . we have a line, the Loman Line. We train a couple of weeks, and put on a couple of exhibitions, see?

WILLY. (*To* LINDA.) That's an idea!

HAPPY. Wait! We form two basketball teams, see? Two water-polo teams. We play each other. It's a million dollars' worth of publicity. Two brothers, see? The Loman Brothers . . . displays in the Royal Palms . . . all the hotels. And banners over the ring and the basketball court—Loman Brothers. Baby, we could sell sporting goods!

WILLY. That is a one-million-dollar idea!

LINDA. Marvelous . . .

BIFF. I'm in great shape as far as that's concerned.

HAPPY. And the beauty of it is, Biff . . . it wouldn't be like a business . . . we'd be out playin' ball again. . . .

BIFF. (*Enthused.*) Yeah, that's . . .

WILLY. Million dollar . . .

HAPPY. And you wouldn't get fed up with it, Biff, it'd be the family again, there'd be the old honor, and comradeship, and if

46

you wanted to go off for a swim or somethin', well, you'd do it! Without some smart cooky gettin' up ahead of you!

WILLY. (*Crosses to above table.* BIFF *crosses to* R. *of* HAPPY.) Lick the world! You guys together could absolutely lick the civilized world.

BIFF. (*At above chair* L. *of table.*) I'll see Oliver tomorrow. Hap, if we could work that out . . .

LINDA. Maybe things are beginning to . . .

WILLY. (*Enthused.*) Stop interrupting! (*To* BIFF.) But don't wear sport-jacket and slacks when you see Oliver.

BIFF. No, I'll . . .

WILLY. (*At above table.*) A business suit, and talk as little as possible, and don't crack any jokes.

BIFF. He did like me; always liked me. . . .

LINDA. He loved you!

WILLY. (*To her.*) Will you stop?! (*She agrees she should, puts hand over mouth, crosses, sits chair over* R. *To* BIFF.) Walk in very serious; you are not applying for a boy's job. Money is to pass—be quiet, fine and serious. Everybody likes a kidder but nobody lends him money.

HAPPY. I'll try to get some myself, Biff; I'm sure I can. . . .

WILLY. I see great things for you kids, I think your troubles are over. But remember, "start big and you'll end big"; ask for fifteen. (*To* LINDA.) Huh? (*To* BIFF.) How much you gonna ask for?

BIFF. Gee, I don't know. . . .

WILLY. (*With a grimace.*) And don't say "Gee." "Gee" is a boy's word. A man walking in for fifteen thousand dollars does not say "Gee!"

BIFF. Ten, I think, would be top, though.

WILLY. "Don't be modest"; you always started too low. Walk in with a big laugh, don't look worried; start off with a couple of your good stories to lighten things up; it's not what you say, it's how you say it—"because personality always wins the day" . . .

LINDA. (*Rises, crosses to* U. R. *corner of table.*) Oliver always thought the highest of him. . . .

WILLY. Will you let me talk?

BIFF. Don't yell at her, Pop, will ya?

WILLY. (*Angering.*) I was talking, wasn't I?

BIFF. (*Crosses below* HAPPY *to foot of stairs.*) I don't like you yelling at her all the time and I'm telling you, that's all.

WILLY. What're you takin' over, this house?

LINDA. Willy . . .

WILLY. (*Turns on her.*) Don't take his side all the time, goddammit!

BIFF. (*Furiously.*) Stop yelling at her!

WILLY. (*Suddenly beaten down, guilt-ridden.*) Give my best to Bill Oliver . . . he may remember me. (*Exits through the bathroom doorway.* HAPPY *crosses slowly* R., *shaking head.*)

LINDA. (*Her voice subdued.*) What'd you have to start that for? (*Crosses* L. *to* BIFF. BIFF *faces her, head down.*) You see how sweet he was as soon as you talked hopefully? Come up and say good night to him. Don't let him go to bed that way.

HAPPY. (*Crosses to above table.*) Come on, Biff, let's buck him up.

LINDA. Please, dear. Just say good night. It takes so little to make him happy. Come. (*She goes into bathroom doorway, calling from within.*) Your pajamas are hanging in the bathroom, Willy!

HAPPY. (*Looking toward where* LINDA *went out.*) What a woman! They broke the mold when they made her. You know that, Biff?

BIFF. (*Crosses to* L. *of chair* L. *of table.*) He's off salary. My God, working on commission!

HAPPY. (*Takes comb from pajama pocket. Combing his hair.*) Well, let's face it; he's no hot-shot selling man. Except that sometimes, you have to admit, he's a sweet personality.

LINDA. (*Entering bedroom and addressing* WILLY *in bathroom. She is straightening bed for him.*) Can you do anything about the shower? It drips.

WILLY. (*From bathroom.*) All of a sudden everything falls to pieces! Goddamn plumbing, oughta be sued!

BIFF. (*Deciding.*) Lend me ten bucks, will ya? I want to buy some new ties.

HAPPY. I'll take you to a place I know. Beautiful stuff. Wear one of my striped shirts tomorrow.

BIFF. She got gray. Mom got awful old. Gee, I'm gonna go in to Oliver tomorrow and knock him for a . . .

HAPPY. Come on up. Tell that to Dad. Let's give him a whirl. Come on.

BIFF. (*Steamed up.*) You know—with ten thousand bucks, boy . . .

HAPPY. That's the talk, Biff, that's the first time I've heard the old confidence out of you! You're gonna live with me, kid, and any babe you want, just say the word. (BIFF *turns away in disgust to refrigerator.* BIFF *and* HAPPY *go toward bedroom after a pause by refrigerator.*)

LINDA. I'm just wondering if Oliver will remember him. You think he might've . . . ?

WILLY. (*Coming out of bathroom in his pajamas. Crosses* D., *sits on bed.* LINDA *takes off his slippers and socks.*) Remember him? What's the matter with you, you crazy? If he'd've stayed with Oliver he'd be on top by now! Wait'll Oliver gets a look at him. You don't know the average caliber any more. The average young man today . . . (*He is getting into bed.* LINDA *crosses to above bed, fixes pillows.*) is got a caliber of zero. Greatest thing in the world for him was to bum around. (BIFF *and* HAPPY *enter bed-room from kitchen.*)

HAPPY. Come on, Biff. (BIFF *follows him.* HAPPY *crosses to* U. L. *corner of bedroom.* LINDA *above bed.*) Pop. (BIFF *crosses* D. *to* L. *of bed, faces front, can't look at* WILLY. BIFF *tries to talk, can't.*)

WILLY. (*Stops short, looking at him.*) Glad to hear it, boy.

HAPPY. He wanted to say good night to you, Sport. (*Pushing* BIFF *a little.*)

WILLY. (*To* BIFF.) Yeah. Knock him dead, boy. What'd you want to tell me?

BIFF. Just take it easy, Pop. Good night. (*Starts out.*)

WILLY. (*Stops* BIFF, *grabbing his arm. Unable to resist.*) And if anything falls off the desk while you're talking to him—like a package or something—don't *you* pick it up. They have office boys for that. . . .

LINDA. I'll make a big breakfast . . .

WILLY. Will you let me finish? (*To* BIFF.) Tell him you were in the business in the West. Not farm work.

BIFF. All right, Dad.

LINDA. I think everything . . .

WILLY. (*Going right through her line.*) And don't under-sell yourself. No less than fifteen thousand dollars.

BIFF. (*Unable to bear him.*) O. K. Good night, Mom. (*Kisses her, exits into kitchen.*)

WILLY. Because you got a greatness in you, Biff, remember that; you got all kindsa greatness . . . (*He lies back, exhausted.*)

LINDA. (*Calling after* BIFF.) Sleep well, darling!

HAPPY. I'm gonna get married, Mom. I wanted to tell you.

LINDA. Go to sleep, dear.

HAPPY. (*Going.*) I just wanted to tell you.

WILLY. Keep up the good work. (BIFF *gets cigarette from top of refrigerator, lights it.* HAPPY *exits up into Boys' Bedroom.* LINDA *sits* U. S. *end of bed beside* WILLY.) God . . . remember that Ebbets' Field game? The championship of the city?

LINDA. Just rest. Should I sing to you?

WILLY. Yeah . . . sing to me. (BIFF *crosses out through kitchen door* L., *then crosses* D. S. *from porch.* LINDA *hums a soft lullaby.*) When that team came out . . . he was the tallest, remember?

LINDA. Oh, yes. . . . And in gold. (LINDA *hums again.* BIFF *stands looking front, thinking.*)

WILLY. (LINDA *slowly looks toward* BIFF.) Like a young god. Hercules . . . something like that. And the sun, the sun all around him. . . . Remember how he waved to me? Right up from the field, with the representatives of three colleges standing by? And the buyers I brought, and the cheers when he came out —Loman, Loman, Loman! God Almighty, he'll be great yet. A star like that, magnificent, can never really fade away! (*Light comes up on the gas heater—furnace.*)

LINDA. (*Timidly, looking toward where* BIFF *is standing.*) Willy, dear, what has he got against you?

WILLY. I'm so tired. Don't talk any more.

LINDA. Will you ask Howard to let you work in New York? (*Furnace heater glows.*)

WILLY. First thing in the morning. Everything'll be all right. (*MUSIC CUE No. 9.* BIFF *puts out cigarette. Crosses back into kitchen, starts upstairs, then he stops. Light comes up full on the water heater.* BIFF *crosses to it, reaches behind it and draws out a length of rubber tubing.* WILLY. *in bed.*) Gee, look at the moon coming between the buildings. (BIFF *is horrified and turns his head toward master bedroom, still dimly lit, winds tube around hand, starts upstairs as* . . .)

CURTAIN

ACT II

SCENE: WILLY, *in shirt sleeves, is sitting chair* R. *of kitchen table, sipping coffee, hat on chair* L. *of table. Coat is hanging on chair over* R. LINDA *is standing above table, dressed in purple cotton dress and apron, watching* WILLY *with a rapt expression as he savors coffee. As he finishes, he motions toward stove. She crosses to stove, brings pot to table, pours cup. Puts pot back on stove.* L. *of* R. *trellis entrance there is a table—i. e., desk for* CHARLEY'S *office—with chair above it.* CURTAIN MU-SIC CUE NO. 10.

WILLY. Wonderful coffee. Meal in itself.

LINDA. (*Eager to send him away in the best of spirits.*) Let me fix you some eggs?

WILLY. No. Take a breath.

LINDA. (*Gets bottle of saccharine from top of refrigerator. Puts saccharine in coffee, stirs it.*) You look so rested, dear. (*Music fades out.*)

WILLY. I slept like a dead one. First time in months. Imagine, sleeping till ten on a Tuesday morning! (*Both laugh.*) Boys left nice and early, heh?

LINDA. They were out of here by eight o'clock.

WILLY. Good work!

LINDA. It was so thrilling to see them leaving together. I can't get over the shaving lotion in this house!

WILLY. (*Smiles.*) Mmm ——

LINDA. Biff was very changed this morning. His whole attitude seemed to be hopeful . . . he couldn't wait to get downtown to see Oliver.

WILLY. He's heading for a change. There's no question, there simply are certain men that take longer to get . . . solidified. How did he dress?

LINDA. His blue suit. He's so handsome in that suit. He could be a . . . anything in that suit!

WILLY. There's no question, no question at all. (*Rises, crosses* R.,

51

ties tie.) Gee, on the way home tonight I'd like to buy some seeds.

LINDA. (*Laughing, enthused.*) That'd be wonderful. But not enough sun gets back there. Nothing'll grow any more.

WILLY. (*Crosses back to her.*) You wait, kid, before it's all over we're gonna get a little place out in the country, and I'll raise some vegetables, a couple of chickens . . .

LINDA. (*With determination.*) You'll do it yet, dear.

WILLY. And they'll get married, and come for a weekend. (*Sudden thought.*) I'd build a little guest-house. . . . 'Cause I got so many fine tools, all I'd need would be a little lumber and some peace of mind. (*Crosses L., looking for coat.*)

LINDA. (*Crosses to chair over R. Gets coat. Joyfully, opening his jacket.*) I sewed the lining. . . . (*Crosses L. to him. He puts, arm in sleeve.*)

WILLY. (*Takes arm out as he starts to talk.*) I could build two guest-houses, so they'd both come. Did he decide how much he's going to ask Oliver for?

LINDA. (*At above chair L. of table.*) He didn't mention it, but I imagine ten or fifteen thousand. You going to talk to Howard today?

WILLY. Yeah. I'll put it to him straight and simple; he'll just have to take me off the road.

LINDA. (*Helping him with his jacket.*) And, Willy, don't forget to ask him for a little advance, because we've got the insurance premium; it's the grace period now.

WILLY. (*Puts arm in again.*) That's a hundred . . . ?

LINDA. (*Lightly.*) A hundred-and-eight, sixty-eight. Because we're a little short again.

WILLY. (*Jrked.*) Why are we short? (*Pulling arm out of coat again.*)

LINDA. (*Apologizing.*) Well, you had the motor job on the car . . .

WILLY. That goddamn Studebaker . . .

LINDA. Well, you got one more payment on the refrigerator . . .

WILLY. But it just broke again. . . .

LINDA. (*Laughing him out of it.*) Well, it's old, dear. . . .

WILLY. I told you we should've bought a well-advertised machine. Charley bought a General Electric and it's twenty years old and it's still good, that son of a bitch!

LINDA. But, Willy . . .

WILLY. Whoever heard of a Hastings refrigerator? Once in my life I would like to own something outright before it's broken! I'm always in a race with the junkyard! I just finished paying for the car and it's on its last legs. The refrigerator consumes belts like a goddamn maniac. They time those things . . . they time them so when you finally paid for them, they're used up. Come on. Come on. (*She holds coat again. He puts it on.*)

LINDA. (*Buttons up his coat, he unbuttons it.*) All told, about two hundred dollars would carry us, dear. But that includes the last payment on the mortgage. After this payment, Willy, the house belongs to us.

WILLY. (*Struck.*) It's twenty-five years?!

LINDA. Biff was nine years old when we bought it.

WILLY. Well . . . that's a great thing. To weather a twenty-five year mortgage is . . .

LINDA. It's an *accomplishment*.

WILLY. (*Crosses L.*) All the cement, the lumber, the reconstruction I put in this house. (*Stamps on floor.*) There ain't a crack to be found in it any more.

LINDA. Well, it served its purpose.

WILLY. What purpose? Some stranger'll come along, move in, and that's that. If only Biff would take this house, and raise a family. (*Starts out.*) I'll be home early. Good-bye, it's late.

LINDA. (*Suddenly remembering.*) Oh, I forgot! (*Getting his hat from chair L. of table, gives it to him. They stop on porch outside kitchen door.*) You're supposed to meet them for dinner.

WILLY. Me?

LINDA. At Frank's Chophouse on 48th near Sixth Avenue.

WILLY. Is that so! How about you?

LINDA. No, just the three of you. They're gonna blow you to a big meal!

WILLY. (*Smiling.*) Don't say! Who thought of that?

LINDA. Biff came to me this morning, Willy, and he said, " Tell Dad we want to blow him to a big meal! " Be there six o'clock. You and your two boys are going to have dinner.

WILLY. Gee whiz. That's really somethin'. I'm gonna knock Howard for a loop, kid. I'll get an advance, and I'll come home with a New York job. Goddammit, now I'm gonna do it.

LINDA. Oh, that's the spirit, Willy!

WILLY. I will never get behind a wheel the rest of my life!

53

LINDA. It's changing, Willy, I can feel it changing.

WILLY. Beyond a question. G'bye, I'm late. . . . (*He starts out* L.)

LINDA. (*Runs* R. *for saccharine on table.*) You got your glasses?

WILLY. (*Feels for them. . . . Comes back in.*) Yeah, yeah, got my glasses. . . .

LINDA. And a handkerchief. . . .

WILLY. Yeah, handkerchief. . . .

LINDA. (*Puts saccharine in his pocket.*) And your saccharine?

WILLY. Yeah, my saccharine.

LINDA. Be careful on the subway stairs. . . . (*Buttoning his coat. His vest is unbuttoned. A silk stocking is seen hanging from her apron pocket.* WILLY *sees it.*)

WILLY. Will you stop mending stockings? At least, while I'm in the house. It gets me nervous. . . . I can't tell you. Please.

LINDA. (*Pushing him out of house.*) Remember, Frank's Chop-house.

WILLY. (*As they cross to* R., *indicating* D. C.) Maybe beets would grow out there.

LINDA. (*Very agreeable.*) But you tried so many times.

WILLY. Yeah, well. . . . Don't work hard today. (*He goes. . . . Exits up* R. *up through trellis.*)

LINDA. Be careful! (*As he vanishes she waves to him. She crosses back into house, looking at garden and shaking head as she crosses back, starts to put dishes away when phone rings. Puts dishes away, then tablecloth on shelf above bedroom steps. To phone.*) I'm coming—in a minute. . . . (*She crosses* R., *lifts it and sits.*) Hello? Oh, Biff!—I'm so glad you called. . . . Yes, sure, I just told him. Yes, he'll be there for dinner at six o'clock. Listen, I was just dying to tell you: you know that little rubber pipe I told you about? That he connected to the gas heater? I finally decided to go down the cellar this morning and take it away and destroy it. But it's gone! Imagine! He took it away himself, it *isn't* there! (*Listens.*) When? Oh, then *you* took it. Oh. . . . Nothing, it's just that I'd hoped he'd taken it away himself. (HOWARD WAGNER *enters* D. L. *pushing typewriter table before him, on which is a wire recorder. He is whistling. Looks around for a place to plug it in. Finds it* D.S. *Then fiddles with it, back to audience.*) Oh, I'm not worried, darling, because this morning he left in such high spirits, it was like the old days!—Did Mr. Oliver see you? Well,

you wait there then. (*She is trembling with sorrow and joy.*) Good-bye, dear, you got your comb? — That's fine. Good-bye, Biff dear. (LINDA *gets up.* WILLY *appears in opening* U. L. HOWARD WAGNER *is thirty-six, fat, and now in his shirt sleeves. He is at typewriter table on which is a wire recorder. He is intent upon threading it. There is a lighted cigar in ashtray on desk.* LINDA *exits into bathroom.*)
WILLY. (*Entering, to* HOWARD. *Hat in hand.*) Pst! Psst! Can I see you a minute, Howard?
HOWARD. (*Businesslike.*) Come in, Willy. Sorry to keep you waiting.
WILLY. (*Crosses, stands* L. *of table, coat unbuttoned, vest buttoned.*) I'd like to have a little talk with you, Howard.
HOWARD. (*Crosses to above table.*) Sure, two minutes. Ever see one of these, Willy?
WILLY. Howard, I want to ask you a little favor. . . .
HOWARD. Most terrific machine I ever saw in my life. I was up all night with it.
WILLY. What is it?
HOWARD. Wire recorder. Just got delivery yesterday. Been driving me crazy.
WILLY. What do you do with it?
HOWARD. I bought it for dictation, but you can do anything with it. Listen to this. . . . I had it home last night . . . listen to what I picked up. The first one is my daughter. Get this. . . . (*Flicks switch* [1] *and we hear " Roll Out the Barrel " being whistled.*) Listen to that kid whistle. (*Moves to* R.)
WILLY. That is lifelike, isn't it?
HOWARD. *Seven years old. Get that tone.*
WILLY. Ts! Ts! (*They listen enraptured. Whistling breaks off.*)
VOICE OF DAUGHTER. " Now you, Daddy."
HOWARD. She's crazy for me! (*Again same song is whistled.*) That's me! — Ha! (*He winks.*)
WILLY. You're very good! (*Whistling breaks off again.*)
HOWARD. Ssh! (*Machine is running silent a moment.*) Get this now, this is my son.
VOICE OF SON. " The capital of Alabama is Montgomery; the capital of Arizona is Phoenix; the capital of Arkansas is Little Rock; the capital of California is Sacramento. . . ." (VOICE *continues reciting.*)

1 Cue is " Phoenix."

55

HOWARD. (*Holding up five fingers.*[1]) Five years old, Willy!

WILLY. He'll make an announcer some day![2]

HIS SON. (*Continuing.*) "The capital of Colorado is Denver; the capital of Connecticut . . ."

HOWARD. Get that—alphabetical order![3] (*Machine breaks off suddenly.*) Wait a minute; the maid kicked the plug out. (*They wait.*)

WILLY. It certainly is a . . .

HOWARD. Ssh . . . for God's sake!

HIS SON. "It's nine o'clock, Bulova watch time. So I have to go to sleep." (HOWARD *picks up cigar from ashtray, gets lighter from pocket.*)

WILLY. That really is . . .

HOWARD. Wait a minute! The next is my wife. (*Lights cigar. They wait.*)

HOWARD'S VOICE. "Go on, say something." (*Pause.*) "Well, you gonna talk?"

HIS WIFE. "I can't think of anything."

HOWARD'S VOICE. "Well, talk—it's turning."

HOWARD. (*Snaps it off.*) That was my wife.

WILLY. That is a wonderful machine. . . .

HOWARD. (*With a challenging tone.*) I tell ya, Willy—I'm gonna take my camera, and my bandsaw, and all my hobbies and out they go. This is the most fascinating relaxation I ever found.

WILLY. I think I'll get one myself.

HOWARD. Sure, they're only a hundred and a half. You can't do without it. Supposing you wanna hear Jack Benny, see? But you can't be home at that hour. So you tell the maid to turn the radio on when Jack Benny comes on, and this automatically goes on with the radio! (*Continues without interruption.*)

WILLY. And when you come home you . . . ?

HOWARD. You can come home twelve o'clock, one o'clock, any time you like, and you get yourself a coke and sit yourself down, throw the switch and there's Jack Benny's program in the middle of the night!

WILLY. I'm definitely going to get one. Because lots of time I'm on the road, and I think to myself, what I must be missing on the radio!

[2] Cue is " Sacramento."
[3] Cue is " Denver."

HOWARD. Don't you have a radio in the car?

WILLY. Well, yeah, but whoever thinks of turning it on?

HOWARD. Say, aren't you supposed to be in Boston?

WILLY. (*Gets chair off* L., *puts it* L. *end of table.*) That's what I want to talk to you about, Howard. You got a minute?

HOWARD. (*Crosses to above table.*) What happened? What're you doing here?

WILLY. Well . . .

HOWARD. (*Not concerned with* WILLY'S *well-being.*) You didn't crack up again, did you?

WILLY. Oh, no, no. . . .

HOWARD. Geez, you had me worried there for a minute. What's the trouble?

WILLY. (*Sits on chair, puts hat under it.*) Well . . . tell you the truth, Howard . . . I've come to the decision that I'd rather not travel any more.

HOWARD. Not travel! Well, what'll you do?

WILLY. (*Definite.*) Remember, Christmas time—when you had the party here? You said you'd try to think of some spot for me here in town.

HOWARD. (*Incredulous.*) With us?

WILLY. Well, sure.

HOWARD. (*Businesslike—drops head.*) Oh, yeah, yeah . . . I remember. Well . . . I couldn't think of anything for you, Willy.

WILLY. I tell ya, Howard . . . the kids are all grown up, y' know. . . . I don't need much any more. If I could take home . . . well, sixty-five dollars a week, I could swing it.

HOWARD. (*Crosses* R. *few steps.*) Yeah, but, Willy, see I . . .

WILLY. I tell ya why, Howard . . . speaking frankly and between the two of us, y' know?—I'm just a little tired. (*Starting to resent having to grovel.*)

HOWARD. (*Crosses to* R. *of table.*) Oh, I could understand that, Willy. (*Businesslike.*) But you're a road man, Willy, and we do a road business. (WILLY *rises.*) We've only got a half dozen salesmen on the floor here.

WILLY. (*Crosses to above table.*) God knows, Howard, I never asked a favor of any man. But I was with the firm when your father used to carry you in here on his arms. . . .

HOWARD. (*Embarrassed and irritated.*) I know that, Willy, but . . .

WILLY. Your father came to me the day you were born and asked me what I thought of the name of Howard, may he rest in peace! (*Crosses to* L. *end of table.*)

HOWARD. I appreciate that, Willy, if I had a spot I'd slam you right in, but I just don't have a single solitary spot. (*Turns, crosses few steps* R. *Pause.*)

WILLY. (*With increasing anger. Swallowing his pride.*) Howard, all I need to set my table is fifty dollars a week.

HOWARD. But where am I going to put you, kid?

WILLY. Look, it isn't a question of whether I can sell merchandise, is it?

HOWARD. No, but it's a business, kid, and everybody's gotta pull his own weight.

WILLY. (*Desperately.*) Just let me tell you a story, Howard. . . .

HOWARD. (*Crosses to table.*) 'Cause you gotta admit, business is business.

WILLY. (*Sits chair* L. *of table.*) Business is definitely business, but just listen for a minute. You don't understand this. When I was a boy . . . eighteen, nineteen, I was already on the road. And there was a question in my mind as to whether selling had a future for me. Because in those days I had a yearning to go to Alaska. See, there were three gold strikes in one month in Alaska, and I felt like going out; just for the ride, you might say.

HOWARD. (*Barely interested.*) Is that so? (*Sits on table* R. *of recorder.*)

WILLY. (*The effect of this speech is to put* HOWARD *in his place.*) Oh, yeah, my father lived many years in Alaska . . . he was an *adventurous* man. . . . We've got quite a little streak of self-reliance in our family. I thought I'd go out with my older brother and try to locate him, and maybe settle in the North with the old man. And I was almost decided to go, when I met a *salesman* in the Parker House. His name was Dave Singleman. And he was eighty-four years old, and he'd drummed merchandise in thirty-one states. And old Dave . . . he'd go up to his room, y' understand, put on his green velvet slippers—I'll never forget—and pick up his phone and call the buyers and without ever leaving his room, at the age of eighty-four, he made his living. And when I saw that, I realized that selling was the greatest career a man could want. 'Cause what could be more satisfying than to be able to go, at the age of eighty-four, into twenty or thirty different cities, and pick up a phone, and be remembered and loved and helped, by so many different people? Do you know; when he died—and by the way he died the *death of a salesman*, in his green velvet slippers in the smoker of the New York, New Haven and Hartford, going into Boston—but when he died, hundreds of salesmen and buyers were at his funeral. Things were sad on a lotta trains for months after that. (*Rises.*) See what I mean? In those days there was personality in it, Howard; there was respect, and comradeship, and gratitude in it. Today, it's all cut and dried, and there's no chance for bringing friendship to bear . . . or personality. They don't know me any more.

HOWARD. (*Angry. Rises, moves away* R.) That's just the thing, Willy. . . .

WILLY. (*Pleading. Crosses* R. *to above* R. *of table.*) If I had *forty* dollars a week . . . that's all I'd need. Forty dollars, Howard.

HOWARD. (*Definite.*) Kid, I can't take blood from a stone, I . . .

WILLY. (*Cuts in. Desperation is on him now.*) Howard, the year Al Smith was nominated your father came to me and . . .

HOWARD. (*Starts off* L.—*to* WILLY, *impatiently.*) I've got to see some people, kid. . . . (WILLY *stops him.*)

WILLY. I'm talking about your *father!* There were promises made in this office! You mustn't tell me you've got people to see —— (*Shouting.*) I put thirty-four years into this firm, Howard, and now I can't pay my insurance! You can't eat the orange and throw the peel away—a man is not a piece of fruit! (*Pause.*) Now pay attention. Your father—in 1928—I had a big year. I averaged a hundred and seventy dollars a week in commissions.

HOWARD. (*Snorts. Turns away.*) Now, Willy, you never averaged . . .

WILLY. (*Bangs his hand on desk.*) I averaged a hundred and seventy dollars a week in the year of 1928! And your father came to me . . . or rather I was in the office here . . . it was right over this desk . . . and he put his hand on my shoulder . . .

HOWARD. Willy, I gotta see some people. Pull yourself together. . . . (*Goes off* L.)

WILLY. (*Facing* R.) Pull myself together! What the hell did I say to him! My God, I was yelling at him! How *could* *I!* . . . ? (*On* HOWARD's *exit the light on his chair grows very bright and strange. MUSIC CUE NO. 10B. Now* WILLY *breaks off, turns staring at it.*

Light occupies the chair, animating it. He approaches this chair, standing across desk from it.) Frank, Frank, don't you remember when I opened up the three new Portland accounts? And you congratulated me long distance? You put your hand on my shoulder, and, Frank . . . (*He leans on desk and with the dead man's name he accidentally puts on switch of recorder and instantly:*)

HOWARD'S SON. ". . . of New York is Albany. The capital of Ohio is Cincinnati, the capital of Rhode Island is . . ." (*And continues.*)

WILLY. (*Leaping away with fright, tries to stop it, then shouts.*) Ha! Howard! Howard! Howard! (*Music fades out.* HOWARD *comes rushing in with his suit coat on.*)

HOWARD. What happened?

WILLY. (*Pointing at machine, which continues nasally, childishly with the capital cities.*) Shut it off, shut it off!

HOWARD. (*Pulls plug out.*) Look, Willy . . .

WILLY. (*Pressing his eyes.*) I gotta get myself some coffee. I'll get some coffee. . . . (*Starts to walk out,* HOWARD *stops him.*)

HOWARD. (*He rolls up cord.*) Willy, look . . .

WILLY. I'll go to Boston.

HOWARD. (*At* L. *end of recorder.*) Willy, you can't go to Boston for us.

WILLY. Why can't I go?

HOWARD. I don't want you to represent us. . . . I've been meaning to tell you for a long time now.

WILLY. Howard . . . are you firing me?

HOWARD. (*Businesslike.*) I think you need a good long rest, Willy. . . .

WILLY. Howard . . .

HOWARD. And when you feel better, come back, and we'll see if we can work something out.

WILLY. (*Crosses to above table.*) But I gotta earn money, Howard. I'm in no position to . . .

HOWARD. Where are your sons? Why don't your sons give you a hand? (*Goes on, barely pausing for* WILLY'S *lines.*)

WILLY. They're working on a very big deal . . .

HOWARD. This is no time for false pride, Willy. You go to your sons and you tell them that you're tired. You've got two great boys, haven't you?

WILLY. Oh, no question, no question, but in the meantime . . .

HOWARD. Then that's that, heh?

WILLY. All right, I'll go to Boston tomorrow.

HOWARD. (*Quietly but final.*) No, no . . .

WILLY. I can't throw myself on my sons—I'm not a cripple!

HOWARD. Look, kid, I'm busy this morning . . .

WILLY. (*Shouts—grabs him.*) Howard, you've got to let me go to Boston!

HOWARD. (*Holding* WILLY *off. Hard, keeping himself under control.*) I've got a line of people to see me this morning. Take five minutes, and pull yourself together, and then go home, will ya? I need the office, Willy. (*Puts chair off* L.) Oh, yeah . . . whenever you can this week, stop by and drop off the samples. You'll feel better, Willy, and then come back and we'll talk. Pull yourself together, kid, there's people outside. (*He pushes table off* L. HOWARD *goes out.* WILLY *stands staring front. Now music is heard.* MUSIC CUE NO. 11—BEN'S *music—first distantly, then closer, closer. . . .* BEN *enters from* U. S. R. *smoking cigarette, puts valise and umbrella on table* L. *of trellis entrance.*)

WILLY. (*Almost a whisper.*) Oh, Ben, how did you do it? What is the answer? Did you wind up the Alaska deal so quickly?

BEN. (*Crosses down, checks watch. Very businesslike.*) Doesn't take much time if you know what you're doing. Just a short business trip; boarding ship in an hour. Wanted to say good-bye.

WILLY. (*Crosses to* C., *stays* U. S. *a little.*) Ben, I've got to talk to you.

BEN. Haven't the time, William. . . .

WILLY. Ben, nothing's working out, I don't know what to do.

BEN. (*Crosses* L. *to* WILLY *at* C.) Now look here, William. I've bought timberland in Alaska and I need a man to look after things for me.

WILLY. God, timberland! Me and my boys in those grand outdoors!

BEN. You've a new continent at your doorstep, William; get out of these cities, they're full of talk and time-payments and courts of law. Screw on your fists and you can fight for a fortune up there.

WILLY. (*Putting on hat. Calling* U. C.) Yes, yes! Linda, Linda! *Music fades out.* LINDA *enters from behind house* U. L. *as of old, with wash.*)

BEN. I haven't much time.

61

WILLY. No, wait!

LINDA. (*Crosses D. below porch.*) Oh, you're back?

WILLY. Linda . . . he's got a proposition for me in Alaska.

LINDA. (*Crosses R. past WILLY. To BEN.*) He's got a beautiful job here. . . . (*Turns. To WILLY.*) But you've got . . .

WILLY. But in Alaska, kid, I could . . .

LINDA. (*Angered.*) You're doing well enough, Willy!

BEN. (*To LINDA.*) Enough for what, my dear?

LINDA. (*Crosses a step toward BEN. Frightened of BEN and angered at him.*) Don't talk those things to him! Enough to be happy right here, right now. (*BEN laughs. To WILLY.*) Why must everybody conquer the world? You're well-liked, and the boys love you, and some day (*To BEN.*) why, old man Wagner told him just the other day that if he keeps it up he'll be a member of the firm, didn't he, Willy? (*BEN laughs.*)

WILLY. (*Crosses R. to BEN. Wagner never did.*) Sure, sure. . . . I am building something with this firm here, Ben, and if a man is building something he must be on the right track, mustn't he?

BEN. What are you building? Lay your hand on it. Where is it?

WILLY. (*Hesitates, then turns to LINDA.*) That's true, Linda, there's nothing!

LINDA. Why? (*To BEN.*) There's a man eighty-four years old . . .

WILLY. That's right, Ben, that's right. When I look at that man I say what is there to worry about . . . ?

BEN. (*Crosses to table.*) Bah!

WILLY. It's true, Ben; all he has to do is go into any city, pick up the phone and he's making his living.

BEN. (*Starts moving R.*) I've got to go. . . .

WILLY. (*Holding BEN back with his speech.*) Why am I wrong?— look at this boy! (*BIFF enters, crosses D. to L. C., exercising, loosing muscles. HAPPY carrying football pants, his shoulder pads and gold helmet. He stays over L. He is wearing baseball cap.*) Without a penny to his name three great universities are begging for him, and from there the sky's the limit, because it's not what you do, Ben. (*BEN stamps out cigarette.*) It's who you know and the smile on your face! It's contacts, Ben, contacts; the whole wealth of Alaska passes over the lunch table at the Commodore Hotel, and that's the wonder, the wonder of this country, that a man can end with diamonds here on the basis of being liked! (*Crosses to BIFF. BEN crosses U. to table, gets umbrella and valise.*) And that's why when you get out on that field today it's important. Because thousands of people will be rooting for you and loving you. (WILLY *crosses to* BEN, *who stops at table.*) And, Ben! When he walks into a business office his name will sound out like a bell and all the doors will open to him! I've seen it, Ben, I've seen it a thousand times! You can't feel it with your hand like timber, but it's there!

BEN. (*Crosses* U. R. *to trellis entrance.*) Good-bye, William.

WILLY. (*Crosses* R. *to* L. *of table over* R. LINDA *follows him.*) Ben . . . am I right? Don't you think I'm right? I value your advice.

BEN. William, you have a new continent up there. You could walk out rich. (*He is gone* U. R.)

WILLY. We'll do it here, Ben! You hear me? We're gonna do it here. (BERNARD *rushes in from* D. L. BIFF *crosses to* L. *MUSIC CUE NO. 12. Repeat MUSIC CUE NO. 4.*)

BERNARD. (*Crosses to* BIFF, *who waves him off.* HAPPY *grabs him.*) Oh, gee, I was afraid you left already!

WILLY. Why? What time is it?

BERNARD. It's half past one!

WILLY. Well, come on, everybody; Ebbets' Field next stop! Where's the pennants? (*He rushes into the house and into bathroom.*)

LINDA. (*To* BIFF.) Did you pack fresh underwear?

BIFF. (*Pacing* D. L. BERNARD *sees* HAPPY *has helmet.*) I got everything. I want to go!

BERNARD. (*At* L. *of* HAPPY.) Hey, Biff, I'm carrying your helmet, ain't I?

HAPPY. No, I'm carrying the helmet.

BERNARD. Oh, Biff, you promised me.

HAPPY. I'm carrying the helmet.

BERNARD. How am I going to get in the locker room?

LINDA. Let him carry the shoulder guards. (*Crosses* U. *into bathroom with wash basket. Changes to coat and hat.*)

BERNARD. Can I, Biff? 'Cause I told everybody I'm going to be in the locker room.

HAPPY. In Ebbets' Field it's the clubhouse.

BERNARD. I meant the clubhouse. (*Music fades out.*)

BERNARD, HAPPY. (*Together.*) Biff! Biff! (*Slight pause.*)

BIFF. (*Like a king.*) Let him carry the shoulder guards. (*MUSIC CUE NO. 12 resumes.*)

HAPPY. (*As he does so, throwing them at him.*) Stay close to us now. (WILLY *rushes in from bathroom with pennants.*)

WILLY. (*Handing all but one of them to* HAPPY.) Everybody wave when Biff comes out on the field. (LINDA *enters kitchen from bathroom, with coat on, carrying hat and purse, stands at door.* HAPPY *and* BERNARD *rush out* U. L. *behind house.*) You set now, boy? (*Crosses to* BIFF.)

BIFF. (*They walk slowly to* D. C.) Ready to go, Pop, every muscle is ready. (*Music fades out.*)

WILLY. You realize what this means?

BIFF. That's right, Pop.

WILLY. (*Feeling* BIFF'S *muscles.*) You're comin' home this afternoon captain of the All-Scholastic championship team of the City of New York.

BIFF. I got it, Pop. And remember, pal, when I take off my helmet, that touchdown is for you.

WILLY. Let's go! (*They start out* U. L. *when* CHARLEY *enters from* U. L., *as of old, in knickers, crosses to* R. *of porch.*) I got no room for you, Charley.

CHARLEY. Room? For what?

WILLY. (*In front of steps.* LINDA *and* BIFF *above* WILLY.) In the car. (WILLY *stops, looks at him.*)

CHARLEY. You goin' for a ride? I wanted to shoot some casino.

WILLY. (*Furious.*) Casino! (*Crosses back step to* CHARLEY. *Incredulously.*) Don't you realize what today is?

LINDA. Oh, he knows, Willy, he's just kidding you.

WILLY. That's nothing to kid about!

CHARLEY. No, Linda, what's goin' on?

LINDA. He's playing in Ebbets' Field. (WILLY *shows him pennant.*)

CHARLEY. Baseball in this weather?

WILLY. Don't talk to him. Come on, come on! (*He is pushing them out.*)

CHARLEY. Wait a minute, didn't you hear the news?

WILLY. What?

CHARLEY. Don't you listen to the radio? Ebbets' Field just blew up

WILLY. Go to hell! (CHARLEY *laughs.*) You! Go to hell! (*Pushing them out. He gives* LINDA *pennant he was carrying.*) Come on, come on, we're late.

CHARLEY. (*Moves* L. *to* WILLY. *As they go* U. L.) Knock a homer, Biff, knock a homer! (WILLY, *last to leave, turns to him.*)

WILLY. I don't think that was funny, Charley. This is the greatest day of his life.

CHARLEY. Willy . . . when are you going to grow up?

WILLY. Yeah, heh? When this game is over, Charley, you'll be laughing out of the other side of your face. They'll be calling him another Red Grange. Twenty-five thousand a year.

CHARLEY. (*Kidding.*) Is that so?

WILLY. Yeah, that's so.

CHARLEY. Well then, Willy, tell me something.

WILLY. What?

CHARLEY. Who is Red Grange?

WILLY. (*Throws* D. *hat, puts up fists.* CHARLEY *ducks under them, runs off* U. L.) Put up your hands. Goddam you, put up your hands! (WILLY *follows him. Traffic sounds outside.*) Who the hell do you think you are, better than everybody else? You don't know everything, you big, ignorant, stupid. . . . Put up your hands! (*Light rises on* R. *side of the stage, on a small table, where* BERNARD, *now mature, stands* D. *stage,* R. C. *facing front. A hat and pair of tennis rackets on table and an overnight bag beside it. This is heard from behind the house during* JENNY'S *and* BERNARD'S *lines:*) What are you walking away for? Don't walk away! If you're going to say something say it to my face! I know you laugh at me behind my back. You'll laugh out of the other side of your goddam face after this game. Touchdown! Touchdown! Eighty thousand people! Touchdown! Right between the goal posts. (BERNARD *is a quiet, earnest, but self-assured young man.* WILLY'S VOICE *is coming from* R. *upstage now. Hearing, he listens toward upstage. Now* JENNY *comes in from* U. R., *his father's secretary.* BERNARD *is smoking cigarette. He is wearing dark blue double-breasted worsted suit, blue shirt, red and blue striped tie, black shoes.*)

JENNY. (*Crosses* D. *in few steps. Distressed, on entering.*) Say, Bernard, will you go out in the hall and . . .

BERNARD. (*Crosses* U. *to* L. *of table.*) What is that noise? Who is it?

JENNY. Mr. Loman. He just got off the elevator.

BERNARD. Who's he arguing with?

JENNY. Nobody. There's nobody with him. I can't deal with him any more, and your father gets all upset every time he comes. I've got a lot of typing to do and your father's waiting to sign it. Will you see him? (*Traffic sounds stop. Backs* U. R. *few steps.* WILLY *enters from behind house* U. R. JENNY *being by this entrance, he sees tennis rackets first, then* JENNY.)

WILLY. (*Gathering his wits.*) Jenny . . . Jenny . . . good to see you. . . . How're ya? Workin'?—or still honest?

JENNY. Fine. . . .

BERNARD. (*Jovial.*) Hello, Uncle Willy. (JENNY *exits* U. R.)

WILLY. (*Almost shocked.*) Bernard! Well, look who's here! (*Crosses to below table.* BERNARD *crosses to him. Comes guiltily to* BERNARD *and warmly shakes his hand.*)

BERNARD. (*Sincere, quiet, modest.*) How are you? Good to see you.

WILLY. What are you doing here?

BERNARD. (*Very friendly.*) Oh, just stopped by to see Pop; get off my feet till my train leaves. I'm going to Washington in a few minutes.

WILLY. Is he in?

BERNARD. Yes, he's in his office with the accountant. (*Crosses to above table, gets chair. Puts it* L. *of table.*) Sit down.

WILLY. (*Sits.*) What're you going to do in Washington?

BERNARD. (*Off-hand.*) Oh, just a case I've got there, Willy.

WILLY. That so? (*Indicating rackets.*) You going to play tennis there?

BERNARD. I'm staying with a friend who's got a court.

WILLY. Don't say! His own tennis court. Must be fine people, I bet.

BERNARD. (*With interest.*) They are, very nice. Dad tells me Biff's in town.

WILLY. (*Big smile.*) Yeah, Biff's in. Working on a very big deal, Bernard.

BERNARD. (*Offers* WILLY *cigarette.*) What's Biff doing?

WILLY. (*Takes silver case, looks at it, but doesn't take cigarette.*) Well, he's been doing very big things in the West. But he decided to establish himself here. Very big. Did I hear your wife had a boy? (*Hands case back.*)

BERNARD. (*Proud but not boasting.*) That's right. Our second.

WILLY. Two boys! What do you know?

BERNARD. What kind of a deal has Biff got?

WILLY. Well, Bill Oliver—very big sporting goods man—called him in from the West. Long distance, carte blanche, special deliveries. Your friends have their own private tennis court?

BERNARD. You still with the old firm, Willy?

WILLY. (*A pause, then.*) I'm . . . I'm overjoyed to see how you made the grade, Bernard, overjoyed. (BERNARD *looks away.*) It's an encouraging thing to see a young man really . . . really . . . Looks very good for Biff. . . . Very. . . . (*He breaks off. Then* . . .) Bernard . . . (*He is so full of emotion, he breaks off again.*)

BERNARD. (*Embarrassed for* WILLY.) What is it, Willy?

WILLY. (*Small and alone, but intense.*) What . . . what's the secret?

BERNARD. (*Knowing what* WILLY *means.*) What secret?

WILLY. How . . . how did you . . . ? Why didn't he ever catch on?

BERNARD. (*Avoiding the issue.*) I wouldn't know that, Willy.

WILLY. (*Looking at* BERNARD. *Confidentially, desperately.*) You were his friend, his boyhood friend —— (BERNARD *crosses slowly to above table.*) There's something I don't understand about it. His life ended after that Ebbets' Field game. From the age of seventeen nothing good ever happened to him.

BERNARD. (*Puts cigarette out in ash-tray.*) He never trained himself for anything.

WILLY. (BERNARD *crosses to above* L. *of* WILLY.) But he did, he did. After high school he took so many correspondence courses. Radio mechanics; television; God knows what, and never made the slightest mark. (*Touches* BERNARD'S *arm.*)

BERNARD. (*Crosses slowly* L. *to* R. C. *Takes off his glasses.*) Willy, do you want to talk candidly?

WILLY. (*Rises, crosses, faces* BERNARD.) I regard you as a very brilliant man, Bernard, I value your advice.

BERNARD. (*Moves* D. R. *past* WILLY, *holding up glasses, looking at them.*) Oh, the hell with the advice, Willy! I couldn't advise you. There's just one thing I've always wanted to ask you. When he was supposed to graduate, and the Math teacher flunked him . . .

WILLY. Oh, that son of a bitch ruined his life!

BERNARD. (*A step.*) Willy, all he had to do was go to summer school and make up that subject.

WILLY. That's right, that's right. . . .

BERNARD. Did you tell him not to go to summer school?

WILLY. Me? I ordered him to go!

BERNARD. Then why wouldn't he go?

WILLY. (*Crosses* U.) Why? Why! Bernard, that question has been trailing me like a ghost for the last fifteen years. He flunked the subject, and laid down and died like a hammer hit him!

BERNARD. (*Crosses* U. *to him.*) Take it easy, kid. . . .

WILLY. Let me talk to you, I got nobody to talk to. Bernard . . . Bernard, was it my fault? Y' see?—it keeps going around in my mind, maybe I did something to him. I got nothing to give him, you see.

BERNARD. (*Not wanting to talk about it. Patting* WILLY.) Don't take it so hard.

WILLY. Why did he lay down? What is the story there?—you were his friend?

BERNARD. (*Crosses* D. R. *few steps.*) Willy . . . I remember, it was June . . . and our grades came out. And he'd flunked math.

WILLY. . . . That son of a bitch . . .

BERNARD. No, Biff was *ready* to enroll in summer school.

WILLY. (*Crosses* D. *Incredible.*) He was?

BERNARD. He wasn't beaten by it at all. But then . . . Willy, he disappeared from the block for almost a month. And I got the idea that —— Did he go up to New England to see you? (WILLY *stares in silence.*) Willy?

WILLY. (*Now with the strong edge of resentment against* BERNARD.) Yeah, he came to Boston. What about it?

BERNARD. (*Crosses to* WILLY.) Well, just that when he came *back* . . . I'll never forget this . . . it always mystifies me. Because I'd thought so well of Biff, even though he'd always taken advantage of me. I loved him, Willy, y' know? And he came back after that month and took his *sneakers*—remember those sneakers with "University of Virginia" printed on them? He was so proud of those, wore them every day. And he took them down in the cellar . . . and *burned them* up in the furnace. We had a fist fight; it lasted at least half an hour. Just the two of us, punching each other down the cellar . . . and crying right through it. . . . I've often thought of how strange it was that I knew right then that he'd given up his life. . . . What happened in Boston, Willy?

(WILLY *looks at him as an intruder. Direct.*) I just bring it up because you asked me.

WILLY. (*Angrily.*) Nothing. . . . What do you mean, "What happened?" What's that got to do with anything?

BERNARD. Well, don't get sore. . . .

WILLY. What are you trying to do, blame it on me? If a boy lays down is that my fault?

BERNARD. Now, Willy, don't get . . .

WILLY. Well, don't . . . don't talk to me that way! What does that mean—"What happened?" (CHARLEY *enters from* U. R. *in vest, light blue shirt, untied bow tie.*)

CHARLEY. (*Crosses to* R. *of table, picks up bag.*) Hey, you're going to miss that train. (*Waves a bottle of bourbon. Crosses above table, puts bag on chair* L. *of table. Opens bag, wraps bottle in pajamas. Puts in bag. Zips it shut.*)

BERNARD. Yeah, I'm going. (*Seeing bottle.*) Thanks, Pop. (*Puts on glasses. Picks up his rackets and hat. Puts on hat.*) Good-bye, Willy, and don't worry about it. You know, "If at first you don't succeed . . ."

WILLY. Yes, I believe in that.

BERNARD. (*Crossing to* WILLY *at* R. C.) But sometimes, Willy, it's better for a man just to walk away.

WILLY. Walk away?

BERNARD. That's right.

WILLY. But if you can't walk away?

BERNARD. (*Sorry for him. After slight pause.*) I guess that's when it's tough. (CHARLEY *turns around to them with bag.*) Good-bye, Willy.

WILLY. (*Very loving.*) Good-bye, boy. (BERNARD *crosses below table to* R. *of* CHARLEY, *takes bag.*)

CHARLEY. (*With arm on* BERNARD'S *shoulder.*) How do you like this kid? Gonna argue a case in front of the Supreme Court.

BERNARD. (*Protesting.*) Pop!

WILLY. (*Genuinely shocked, pained, and happy.*) No! The Supreme Court!

BERNARD. I gotta run. 'Bye, Dad!

CHARLEY. Knock 'em dead, Bernard! (BERNARD *goes off* U. R.)

WILLY. (*As* CHARLEY *takes out his wallet.*) The Supreme Court—and he didn't even mention it.

CHARLEY. (*Not gloating.*) He don't have to—he's gonna *do* it. (*Crossing* U. *to above chair* L. *of table.*)

WILLY. (*Crosses slowly to far* R.) And you never told him what to do. Did you? You never took any interest in him.

CHARLEY. (*Takes out his wallet.*) My salvation is that I never took any interest in anything. There's some money, fifty dollars. I got an accountant inside. (*Crosses to above table. He starts to pull some bills out of wallet, but* WILLY'S *line stops him.*)

WILLY. Charley, look . . . (*Crosses* U. *with difficulty.*) I got my insurance to pay. . . . If you can manage it . . . I need a hundred and ten dollars. (CHARLEY *doesn't reply for a moment— merely stops moving.*) I'd draw it from my bank, but Linda would know, and I . . .

CHARLEY. (*Putting chair out* L. *of table.*) Sit down, Willy.

WILLY. (*Moves toward chair* L.) I'm keeping an account of everything, remember.

CHARLEY. Willy . . .

WILLY. I'll pay every penny back. (*He sits.*)

CHARLEY. Now listen to me, Willy.

WILLY. I want you to know I appreciate . . .

CHARLEY. (*Sits on table between chair and table.*) Willy, what're you doin'? What the hell is goin' on in your head?

WILLY. Why, I'm simply . . .

CHARLEY. I offered you a job. You can make fifty dollars a week . . . and I won't send you on the road.

WILLY. I've got a job. . . .

CHARLEY. Without pay? What kind of a job is a job without pay? (*Rises, moves above to* L. *of* WALLY.) Now look, kid, enough is enough. I'm not a genius but I know when I'm being insulted.

WILLY. Insulted?

CHARLEY. Why don't you want to work for me?

WILLY. What's the matter with you? I've got a job.

CHARLEY. Then what're you walkin' in here every week for?

WILLY. Well, if you don't want me to walk in here . . .

CHARLEY. I am offering you a job.

WILLY. (*Rises, moves* L.) I don't want your goddam job!

CHARLEY. When the hell are you going to grow up?

WILLY. (*Turns, furious.*) You big ignoramus, if you say that to me again I'll rap you one! I don't care how big you are! (*Moves* D. C. *He's ready to fight. Pause.* CHARLEY *crosses* R. *few steps.*)

70

CHARLEY. (*Crosses* L. *to* WILLY. *Kindly, going to him.*) How much do you need, Willy?

WILLY. I'm strapped, Charley, I'm strapped. I was just fired.

CHARLEY. (*Hating* HOWARD.) Howard fired you?

WILLY. That snotnose! Imagine that! I named him. I named him Howard.

CHARLEY. (*Hand on* WILLY'S *arm.*) Willy . . . when're you gonna realize that . . . ? You named him Howard, but you can't sell that. The only thing you got in this world is what you can sell. And the funny thing is that you're a salesman, and you don't know that.

WILLY. (*Proud. Fumbling.*) I've always tried to think otherwise. I always felt that if a man was impressive, and well liked, that nothing . . .

CHARLEY. Why must everybody like you? Who liked J. P. Morgan? Was he impressive? In a Turkish bath he looked like a butcher. But with his pockets on he was very well liked. Now listen, Willy—I know you don't like me—and nobody can say I'm in love with you, but I'll give you a job because . . . just for the hell of it, put it that way. Now what do you say?

WILLY. I . . . I just can't work for you, Charley.

CHARLEY. What're you, jealous of me?

WILLY. I can't work for you, that's all, don't ask me why.

CHARLEY. (*Crosses* R. *Angered, takes out more bills.*) You been jealous of me all your life, you damned fool! (*Crosses back to* WILLY.) Here, pay your insurance.

WILLY. I'm keeping strict accounts.

CHARLEY. I've got some work to do. Take care of yourself. (*Gives him bills.*) And pay your insurance. (*Crosses* U., *puts chair alongside table.*)

WILLY. (*Moving to* R.) Funny, y' know? After all the highways, and the trains and the appointments, and the years, you end up worth more dead than alive.

CHARLEY. Willy . . . nobody's worth nothin' dead. (*Slight pause,* WILLY *is moving* D. S. *over* R.) Did you hear what I said? (WILLY *crosses* U., *dreaming.*) Willy!

WILLY. (*Crosses to* R. *of table.*) Apologize to Bernard for me when you see him. I didn't mean to argue with him . . . he's a fine boy. They're all fine boys . . . and they'll end up *big* . . .

all of them. . . . Some day, they'll all play tennis together. Wish me luck, Charley . . . he saw Bill Oliver today.

CHARLEY. Good luck.

WILLY. (*On verge of tears.*) Charley . . . you're the only friend I got. . . . Isn't that a remarkable thing? (*He goes out* U. R.)

CHARLEY. Jesus! (CHARLEY *stares after him a moment and exits* D. R. *MUSIC CUE NO. 12C.* STANLEY, *a young waiter, appears from up* R., *carrying a table, followed by* HAPPY, *who is carrying two chairs. Table, which was used as* CHARLEY'S *desk, is now used as 2d table for restaurant scene. He is wearing tan shirt with brown and green tie, double-breasted brown glen-plaid suit and brown oxfords.*)

STANLEY. (*Putting table down* D. R.) That's all right, Mr. Loman, I can handle it myself. (*He turns and takes chairs from* HAPPY *and places them at table, one on* L. *and one on* R. *Music fades out.*)

HAPPY. (*Crosses* L., *then back to* R. *of table. Glancing around.*) Oh, this is better. (*Sits* R. *of table.*)

STANLEY. Sure, in the front there you're in the middle of all kindsa noise. (*Crosses to other [desk] table above and a little* L. *Puts juke-box lamp on it that he got from lower shelf on above side of desk.*) Whenever you got a party, Mr. Loman, you just tell me and I'll put you back here. (*Gets table-cloth from shelf, crosses* D., *spreads it on* HAPPY'S *table.*) Y' know, there's a lotta people they don't like it private, because when they go out they like to see a lotta action around them, because they're sick and tired to stay in the house by theirself. But I know you, you ain't from Hackensack. You know what I mean? (*Crosses* U., *gets napkin.*)

HAPPY. So how's it coming, Stanley?

STANLEY. (*Crosses* D., *puts napkin on* HAPPY'S *table.*) Ah, it's a dog's life. I only wish during the war they'd 'a' took me in the army.—I coulda been dead by now. (*Crosses* U., *gets menu and ash-tray.*)

HAPPY. My brother's back, you know.

STANLEY. (*Crosses back.*) Oh, he come back, heh? From the Far West?

HAPPY. Yeah, big cattle man, my brother, so treat him right. And my father's coming too. . . .

STANLEY. Oh, your father too! (*Offers menu.*)

72

HAPPY. You got a couple of nice lobsters?

STANLEY. (*At above table.*) Hundred percent big.

HAPPY. I want them with the claws.

STANLEY. Don't worry, I don't give you no mice. (HAPPY *laughs.*)
How about some wine? It'll put a head on the meal.

HAPPY. No . . . you remember, Stanley, that recipe I brought
you from overseas? With the champagne in it?

STANLEY. Oh, yeah, sure. I got it tacked up yet in the kitchen.
But that'll have to cost a buck apiece anyways.

HAPPY. That's all right.

STANLEY. What'd you, hit a *number or somethin'*?

HAPPY. (*Confidential.*) No, it's a little celebration. My brother
is . . . (*Puts cigarette in mouth.*) I think he pulled off a big deal
today. I think we're going into business together.

STANLEY. (*Confidential, too.*) Great! That's the best for you.
Because a family business, you know what I mean?—that's the
best.

HAPPY. That's what I think.

STANLEY. (*Lights* HAPPY's *cigarette.*) 'Cause what's the difference,
somebody steals?—It's in the family, know what I mean? (HAPPY
laughs.)

HAPPY. (*Raises his head.*) Sh! (*Closes eyes, looking front.*)

STANLEY. What?

HAPPY. You notice I wasn't lookin' right or left, was I?

STANLEY. No.

HAPPY. And my eyes are closed?

STANLEY. So what's the . . . ?

HAPPY. Strudel's comin'.

STANLEY. (*Catching on, looks around.*) Ah, no, there's no . . .
(*Breaks off, looking off. A furred, lavishly dressed girl* [MISS
FORSYTHE] *enters,* U. R. *Crosses to* L. *and below 2d table. Both
follow her with their eyes. She puts bag on table. Takes off gloves,
looking over* HAPPY's *head.*) Jeez, how'd ya know?

HAPPY. I got radar or something. (*Lifting* STANLEY's R. *arm. looking under it. Staring directly at her profile.*) Oooooooooo . . .
Stanley!

STANLEY. I think that's for you, Mr. Loman. (GIRL *removes fur
piece.*)

HAPPY. Look at that mouth. Oh, God! And the binoculars.

STANLEY. Jeez, you got a life, Mr. Loman. (GIRL *sits* L. *of table, pulling chair forward.*)

HAPPY. Wait on her. (*Gives* STANLEY *menu.*)

STANLEY. (*Going to* GIRL'S *table.*) Would you like a menu, ma'am?

GIRL. I'm expecting someone, but I'd like a . . .

HAPPY. Why don't you bring her . . . ? Excuse me, Miss, do you mind? I sell champagne, and I'd like you to try my brand. Bring her a champagne, Stanley. (STANLEY *puts menu on shelf of* GIRL'S *table.*)

GIRL. That's awfully nice of you.

HAPPY. Don't mention it. It's all company money. (*Laughs. She laughs.* STANLEY *laughs. She freezes him with a look. He exits.* HAPPY *deliberately knocks cigarettes off his table towards her, says " oops " and laughs.*)

GIRL. That's a charming product to be selling, isn't it?

HAPPY. (*Rises, crosses above to her* R.) Oh, gets to be like everything else. Selling is selling, y' know.

GIRL. I suppose.

HAPPY. (*Kneeling on chair above his table.*) You don't happen to sell, do you?

GIRL. No, I don't sell. (*He picks up cigarettes and straddles his chair, facing her.*)

HAPPY. Would you object to a compliment from a stranger? (*She looks at him, a little arch.*) You ought to be on a magazine cover.

GIRL. I have been. (STANLEY *comes on with a glass of champagne.*)

HAPPY. What'd I say before, Stanley?—you see?—She's a cover girl.

STANLEY. Huh—oh, yeah, sure, sure. (*At above her table, serves her champagne.*)

GIRL. (*Takes drink.*) Thank you.

HAPPY. You know what they say in France, don't you? " Champagne is the drink of the complexion." . . . H'ya, Biff! (*Rises, steps to above his table.* BIFF, *wearing blue shirt, black tie, single-breasted blue-gray gabardine suit, has entered and crosses* D. *to* R. *of* R. *table.* STANLEY *gets napkin from shelf of* L. *table, brings it* D. *to* R. *table for* BIFF. *Crosses up to* R. *of* L. *table.*)

BIFF. Hello, kid, sorry I'm late.

HAPPY. I just got here. Uh, Miss . . .

GIRL. Forsythe.

HAPPY. Miss Forsythe, this is my brother.

BIFF. Is Dad here? (*Sits* R. *of table.*)

HAPPY. His name is Biff. You might've heard of him? Great football player. (BIFF *lights cigarette.*)

GIRL. Really? What team?

HAPPY. Are you familiar with football?

GIRL. No, I'm afraid not.

HAPPY. (*With authority.*) Biff is quarterback with the New York Giants. (BIFF *looks at* HAPPY, *then at* GIRL.)

GIRL. Well!—that is nice, isn't it? (*She drinks.*)

HAPPY. Good health.

GIRL. I'm happy to meet you.

HAPPY. That's my name, Hap. It's really Harold, but at West Point they called me Happy.

GIRL. (*Now really impressed.*) Oh . . . I see. How do you do? (*She turns, gets cigarette from bag.* STANLEY *crosses between her and* HAPPY *and lights her cigarette.*)

BIFF. Isn't Dad coming?

HAPPY. You want her?

BIFF. Oh, I could never make that.

HAPPY. I remember the time that idea would never come into your head. . . . Where's the old confidence, Biff?

BIFF. . . . I just saw Oliver . . .

HAPPY. Wait a minute. I've got to see that old confidence again. Do you want her? She's on call.

BIFF. Oh, no —— (*Looks at* GIRL.)

HAPPY. Watch this. . . . (*He turns to* GIRL. *In a certain direct tone.*) Honey? (*She turns to him.*) Are you busy?

GIRL. Well, I am . . . (*She pauses, he takes a deliberate drag of his cigarette.*) but I could make a phone call.

HAPPY. (*As she takes notebook from handbag.*) Do that, will you, honey? And see if you can get a friend. We'll be here for a while. Biff is one of the greatest football players in the country.

GIRL. (*Stands, looking frightened.*) Well, I'm certainly happy to meet you.

HAPPY. Come back soon.

GIRL. I'll try.

HAPPY. (*An order.*) Don't try, honey, try hard. (*She picks up handbag, exits.* STANLEY *follows with champagne glass, shaking*

75

his head in bewildered admiration. Sits L. *of table.*) Isn't that a shame now? A beautiful girl like that? That's why I can't get married. There's not a good woman in a thousand. . . .

BIFF. Hap, look . . .

HAPPY. I told you she was on call!

BIFF. Cut it out, will ya? I want to say something to you.

HAPPY. Did you see Oliver?

BIFF. (*With self-hate.*) I saw him all right. Now look, I want to tell Dad a couple of things and I want you to help me.

HAPPY. What? Is he going to back you?

BIFF. Are you crazy? You're out of your goddam head, you know that?

HAPPY. Why? What happened?

BIFF. I did a terrible thing today, Hap. It's been the strangest day I ever went through. I'm all numb, I swear.

HAPPY. You mean he wouldn't see you?

BIFF. Well, I waited six hours for him, see? All day kept sending my name in.

HAPPY. He remembered you, didn't he?

BIFF. (*Stops* HAPPY *with a gesture.*) Finally, about five o'clock he comes out, didn't remember who I was or anything. . . . I felt like such an idiot, Hap. . . .

HAPPY. Did you tell him my Florida idea?

BIFF. He walked away. I saw him for one minute.—How the hell did I ever get the idea I was a salesman there? I even believed myself that I'd been a salesman for him! And then he gave me one look and—I realized—we've been talking in a dream for fifteen years . . . I was a shipping clerk.

HAPPY. What'd you do?

BIFF. (*With great tension and wonder.*) Well, he left, see. And the secretary went out. I was all alone in the waiting-room. I felt so mad I could've torn the walls down. I don't know what came over me, y' know? The next thing I know I'm in his office . . . panelled walls, everything. I can't explain it . . . I . . . Hap, I took his fountain-pen. (*Feeling pen under his coat.*)

HAPPY. Jeez, did he catch you?

BIFF. Then I ran out. . . . I ran down all eleven flights. . . . I ran and ran . . .

HAPPY. That was awful dumb . . . what'd you do that for?

BIFF. (*Agonized.*) I don't know, I just . . . wanted to take something, I don't know. You gotta help me, Hap, I'm gonna tell Pop.

HAPPY. You crazy? What for?

BIFF. Hap, he's got to understand that I'm not the man somebody lends that kind of money to. He thinks I've been spiting him all these years and it's eating him up. . . .

HAPPY. That's just it. You tell him something nice. . . .

BIFF. I can't. . . .

HAPPY. (*Rises, crosses to above table.*) Say you got a lunch date with Oliver tomorrow. . . .

BIFF. So what do I do tomorrow?

HAPPY. You leave the house tomorrow and come back at night and say Oliver is thinking it over. And he thinks it over for a couple of weeks, and gradually it fades away and nobody's the worse.

BIFF. But it'll go on forever!

HAPPY. Dad is never so happy as when he's looking forward to something. (*WILLY enters and HAPPY, seeing him, cuts BIFF off.*) Hullo, scout! (*HAPPY takes WILLY's hat.*)

WILLY. Gee, I haven't been here in years! (*STANLEY has followed WILLY in and sets chair for him above table. He starts off, but HAPPY stops him.*)

HAPPY. Stanley! (*STANLEY stands by, waiting for order.*)

BIFF. (*Indicating chair L. of table.*) Sit down, Pop . . . you want a drink?

WILLY. Sure, I don't mind.

BIFF. Let's get a load on.

WILLY. You look worried.

BIFF. No—no. . . . (*To STANLEY.*) Scotch all around, make it doubles. (*Sits R. of table.*)

STANLEY. Doubles, right. (*He goes.*)

WILLY. You had a couple already, didn't you? (*Sits L. of table. HAPPY puts WILLY's hat under L. chair.*)

BIFF. (*HAPPY sits above table.*) Just a couple, yeah.

WILLY. Well, what happened, boy? (*Nodding affirmatively, with a smile.*) Everything go all right?

BIFF. (*Takes a breath, then.*) Pal . . . (*He is smiling bravely, and WILLY is smiling.*) I had an experience today.

HAPPY. Terrific, Pop.

WILLY. That so? What happened?

BIFF. (*High, slightly alcoholic, above the earth.*) I'm going to tell you everything from first to last. It's been a strange day. (*Silence. He composes himself as best he can, but his breath keeps breaking the rhythm of his voice.*) I had to wait quite a while for him, and . . .

WILLY. Oliver . . . ?

BIFF. (*Remembering.*) Yeah, Oliver. All day, as a matter of cold fact. And a lot of . . . instances . . . facts, Pop; facts about my life came back to me. Who was it, Pop . . . (*Gently.*) who ever said I was a salesman with Oliver?

WILLY. Well, you were. . . .

BIFF. No, Dad, I was a *shipping clerk.*

WILLY. But you were practically . . .

BIFF. (*With determination.*) Dad, I don't know who said it first, but I was never a salesman for Bill Oliver.

WILLY. What're you talking about?

BIFF. Let's hold on the facts tonight, Pop, we're not going to get anywhere bullin' around; I was a shipping clerk!

WILLY. (*Angered.*) All right, now listen to me. . . .

BIFF. Why don't you let me finish?

WILLY. (*With impatience.*) I'm not interested in any stories about the past or any crap of that kind because the woods are burning, boys, you understand? There's a big blaze going on all around; I was fired today.

BIFF. (*Shocked.*) How could you be . . . ?

WILLY. I was fired, and I'm looking for a little good news to tell your mother, because the woman has waited and the woman has suffered. The gist of it is that I haven't got a story left in my head, Biff. So don't give me a lecture about facts and aspects. I am not interested. Now what've you got to say to me? (STANLEY *enters with three drinks.* BIFF *drinks his immediately. They wait until* STANLEY *leaves.*) Did you see Oliver?

BIFF. Jesus, Dad!

WILLY. You mean you didn't go up there?

HAPPY. Sure, he went up there.

BIFF. I did . . . I . . . saw him. How could they fire you?

WILLY. (*On edge of his chair.*) What kind of a welcome did he give you?

BIFF. He won't even let you work on commission?

WILLY. I'm out! (*Driving.*) So tell me, he gave you a warm welcome?

HAPPY. Sure, Pop, sure!

BIFF. (*Driven.*) Oh, well, it was kind of . . .

WILLY. I was wondering if he'd remember you. (*To* HAPPY.) Imagine, man doesn't see him for ten twelve years and gives him that kind of a welcome!

HAPPY. Damn right!

BIFF. (*Trying to return to the offensive.*) Pop, look . . .

WILLY. You know why he remembered you, don't you? Because you impressed him in those days.

BIFF. Let's talk quietly and get this down to the facts, huh?

WILLY. (*As though* BIFF *had been interrupting.*) Well, what happened? It's great news, Biff; did he take you into his office or'd you talk in the waiting room?

BIFF. Well, he came in, see, and . . .

WILLY. (*Big smile.*) What'd he say?—betcha he threw his arm around you!

BIFF. Well, he kinda . . .

WILLY. He's a fine man. (*To* HAPPY.) Very hard man to see, y' know.

HAPPY. (*Agreeing.*) Oh, I . . . [know].

WILLY. (*To* BIFF.) Is that where you had the drinks?

BIFF. . . . Yeah, he gave me a couple of . . . no, no . . . !

HAPPY. (*Cutting in.*) He told him my Florida idea.

WILLY. Don't interrupt. (*To* BIFF.) How'd he react to the Florida idea?

BIFF. Dad, will you give me a minute to explain?

WILLY. (*Annoyed.*) I've been waiting for you to explain since I sat down here! What happened; he took you into his office, and what?

BIFF. Well . . . I talked . . . and . . . and he listened, see . . .

WILLY. Famous for the way he listens, y' know. What was his answer?

BIFF. His answer was . . . (*Breaks off. He is suddenly angry.*) Dad, you're not letting me tell you what I want to tell you!

WILLY. (*Accusing, angered.*) You didn't see him, did you?

BIFF. I did see him!

WILLY. What'd you, insult him or something? You insulted him, didn't you?

BIFF. Listen, will you let me out of it, will you just let me out of it!

79

HAPPY. What the hell?

WILLY. Tell me what happened?

BIFF. (*To* HAPPY.) I can't talk to him! (*MUSIC CUE NO.* 12D.)

YOUNG BERNARD. (*Dressed in knickers, enters from* U. L. *Rapping on kitchen door.*) Mrs. Loman, Mrs. Loman!

HAPPY. Tell him what happened!

BIFF. (*To* HAPPY. *Rises, crosses few steps* R.) Shut up and leave me alone!

WILLY. No, no! You had to go and flunk Math! (BERNARD *crosses* D. *in front of porch outside kitchen* L.)

BIFF. What Math? What're you talking about?

BERNARD. (D. S., *turns up to house.*) Mrs. Loman, Mrs. Loman!

WILLY. (*Wildly.*) Math, Math, Math!

BIFF. (*Crosses to* R. *of table.*) Take it easy, Pop. . . .

BERNARD. Mrs. Loman! (*Crosses* U. *to door.*)

WILLY. (*Furious.*) If you hadn't flunked you'd've been set by now!

BIFF. (*Sits* R. *of table.*) Now look, I'm gonna tell you what happened and you're going to listen to me.

BERNARD. (*Opens kitchen door, enters.*) Mrs. Loman!

BIFF. I waited six hours . . .

HAPPY. What the hell are you saying?

BIFF. I kept sending in my name but he wouldn't see me. So finally he . . . (LINDA *enters kitchen from bathroom as of old.* BIFF *continues unheard.*)

BERNARD. Biff flunked Math!

LINDA. No!

BERNARD. Birnbaum flunked him! They won't graduate him! (*During this* BIFF *takes out fountain-pen and pantomimes what happened to him.*)

LINDA. But they have to. He's gotta go to the university. (*Crosses out to below steps,* L. *of kitchen door.*) Where is he? Biff! Biff!

BERNARD. (*Crosses* D. *to her* L.) No, he left, he went to Grand Central.

LINDA. Grand . . . You mean he went to Boston! (*Crosses* U. *to door.*)

BERNARD. (*Following her.*) Is Uncle Willy in Boston?

LINDA. Oh, maybe Willy can talk to the teacher. (*Exits into bathroom.*) Oh, the poor, poor boy! (BERNARD *exits* U. L.)

BIFF. (*At table now, audible, holding up fountain-pen.*) . . . so

I'm washed up with Oliver, you understand? Are you listening to me?

WILLY. (*At a loss.*) Yeah, sure . . . if you hadn't flunked . . .

BIFF. Flunked what? What're you talking about?

WILLY. Don't blame everything on me! I didn't flunk Math—you did! What pen?

HAPPY. That was awful dumb, Biff, a pen like that is worth . . .

WILLY. (*Seeing pen for first time.*) You took Oliver's pen?

BIFF. (*Weakening.*) Dad, I just explained it to you. . . .

WILLY. (*Picks up pen.*) You stole Bill Oliver's fountain-pen!?

BIFF. I didn't exactly steal it! . . . That's just what I've been explaining to you!

HAPPY. He had it in his hand and just then Oliver walked in, so he got nervous and stuck it in his pocket!

WILLY. (*Tosses pen on table.*) My God, Biff!

BIFF. I never intended to do it, Dad!

OPERATOR'S VOICE. (*Off* L., *over loud speaker.*) Standish Arms, good evening!

WILLY. (*Shouting off* L.) I'm not in my room!

BIFF. (*Rises, frightened.*) Dad, what's the matter?

OPERATOR. Ringing Mr. Loman for you!

WILLY. (*Starts to rise.*) I'm not there, stop it!

BIFF. (HAPPY *rises, holds* WILLY D.) Dad, I'll make good, I'll make good. Sit down, now. . . .

WILLY. No, you're no good, you're not good for anything. . . .

BIFF. (*Kneels in front of* WILLY.) I am, Dad, I'll find something else, you understand? Now don't worry about anything. (*Holds up* WILLY's *face.*) Talk to me, Dad.

OPERATOR. Mr. Loman does not answer. Shall I page him?

WILLY. No, no, no . . .

HAPPY. He'll strike something, Pop.

WILLY. No, no . . .

BIFF. (*Desperately, grasping* WILLY's *arms.*) Pop, listen . . . listen to me, I'm telling you something good. Oliver talked to his partner about the Florida idea. You listening? He . . . he talked to his partner, and he came to me. . . . I'm going to be all right, you hear? Dad, listen to me, he said it was just a question of the amount!

WILLY. Then you . . . got it?

HAPPY. He's gonna be terrific, Pop!

WILLY. (*Takes* BIFF'S *head between hands, tries to rise.*) Then you got it, haven't you? You got it!? You got it!?
BIFF. (*He and* HAPPY *hold* WILLY *in chair. Agonized.*) No—no, look, Pop! (*Crosses to* R. *of table.*) I'm supposed to have lunch with them tomorrow. . . . I'm just telling you this so you'll know that I can still make an impression, Pop, and I'll make good somewhere, but I can't go tomorrow, see?
WILLY. Why not? You simply . . .
BIFF. But the pen, Pop . . .
WILLY. You give it to him and tell him it was an oversight!
HAPPY. Sure, have lunch tomorrow!
BIFF. I can't say that . . .
WILLY. You were doing a crossword puzzle and accidentally used his pen!
BIFF. (*Aware that* WILLY *is wandering.*) Listen, kid, I took those balls years ago, now I walk in with his fountain pen! That clinches it, don't you see? I can't face him like that! I'll try elsewhere. . . .
PAGE'S VOICE. (*Loud speaker off* L.) Paging Mr. Loman!
WILLY. Don't you want to be anything!
BIFF. Pop, how can I go back?
WILLY. You don't want to be anything, is that what's behind it?
BIFF. (*Now angering at* WILLY *for not crediting his sympathy. Leaning across table.*) Don't take it that way! You think it was easy to walk into that office after what I'd done to him? A team of horses couldn't have dragged me back to Bill Oliver!
WILLY. Then why'd you go?
BIFF. Why did I go? Why did I go? Look at you! Look at what's become of you! (*Off* L. WOMAN *laughs.*)
WILLY. Biff, you're going to go to that lunch tomorrow or . . .
BIFF. I can't go. I've got no appointment!
HAPPY. Biff, for . . . !
WILLY. Are you spiting me? (*Slaps* BIFF.)
BIFF. Don't take it that way! Goddammit! (*Crosses to below table.*)
WILLY. (*Rises.* HAPPY *gets between them.*) You rotten little louse! Are you spiting me?!
WOMAN. (*Off* L.) Someone's at the door, Willy!
BIFF. I'm no good, can't you see what I am!?
HAPPY. (*Walking* WILLY L. *to* C.) Hey, you're in a restaurant!

82

Now cut it out, both of you! (BIFF *leans heavily on table, standing below it.* MISS FORSYTHE *and* LETTA *enter to them.* BIFF *crosses* R.) Hello, girls, sit down. (*Crosses to above* L. *chair of* R. *table.* WOMAN *laughs off* L.)

MISS FORSYTHE. I guess we might as well. This is Letta. (WILLY *unties necktie, unbuttons his vest. Pushes her to chair above* R. *table. Then crosses above to* L. *of* L. *table.* BIFF *crosses to* R. *of* R. *table.*)

WOMAN. (*Off* L.) Willy, are you going to wake up?

HAPPY. How're ya, Miss, sit down. . . . What do you drink? (LETTA *sits above* R. *table.*)

MISS FORSYTHE. (*Picking up fur, gloves.*) Letta might not be able to stay long.

LETTA. I gotta get up very early tomorrow. I got jury duty. I'm so excited! Were you fellows ever on a jury?

BIFF. No, but I been in front of them! (*Girls laugh.*) This is my father.

LETTA. Sit down with us, Pop.

HAPPY. Sit him down, Biff!

BIFF. (*Crosses below, gets drink. Going to him.*) Come on, slugger, drink us under the table. To hell with it! (WILLY *drinks.* BIFF *takes him to chair* L. *of* R. *table.*) Come on, sit down, pal. (*On* BIFF'S *last insistence* WILLY *has been about to sit.*)

WOMAN. (*Now urgently.*) Willy, are you going to answer the door! (WOMAN'S *call pulls him back. He rises, starts* R. *and then* U. S., *befuddled.*)

BIFF. Hey, where are you going?

WILLY. Open the door.

BIFF. The door?

WILLY. . . . The washroom . . . the door . . . where's the door?

BIFF. (*Leading* WILLY *to* L.) Just go straight down. (WILLY *moves* L. *and exits.*)

WOMAN. Willy, Willy, are you going to get up, get up, get up, get up!

LETTA. I think it's wonderful you bring your Daddy along. (HAPPY *sits* L. *of* R. *table.*)

MISS FORSYTHE. Oh, he isn't really your father!

BIFF. (*At* L., *turning to her. Crosses slowly to her.*) Miss Forsythe, you've just seen a prince walk by. A fine, troubled prince.

83

A hardworking, unappreciated prince. A pal . . . you under-stand? A good companion. Always for his boys.

LETTA. That's so sweet.

HAPPY. Well, girls, what's the program? We're wasting time. Come on, Biff. Gather around. Where would you like to go?

BIFF. (*Crosses R. to above R. table.* LETTA *rises, crosses above him to R. of L. table.*) Why don't you do something for him?

HAPPY. Me!

BIFF. Don't you give a damn for him, Hap?

HAPPY. What're you talking about? I'm the one who . . .

BIFF. I sense it, you don't give a good goddamn about him. (*Takes rolled-up hose from his pocket and puts it on table in front of* HAPPY.) Look what I found in the cellar, for Christ's sake. How can you bear to let it go on?

HAPPY. Me? Who goes away? Who runs off and . . . ?

BIFF. Yeah, but he doesn't mean anything to you—you could help him, I can't! Don't you understand what I'm talking about? He's going to kill himself, don't you know that?

HAPPY. Don't I know it! Me!

BIFF. Hap . . . help him. . . . Jesus . . . help him. . . . Help me, help me, I can't bear to look at his face! (*Ready to weep, he picks up tube, hurries out up R.* STANLEY *enters, crosses above to L. of L. table. Puts chair above it. Puts lamp on shelf of table.*)

HAPPY. (*Starting after him.*) Where are you going?

MISS FORSYTHE. What's he so mad about? (*Crosses R.*)

HAPPY. Come on, girls, we'll catch up with him.

MISS FORSYTHE. (*As he pushes her out.*) Say, I don't like that temper of his!

HAPPY. (*Crosses D. to R. table, gets pen, then U. to exit.*) He's just a little overstrung, he'll be all right!

WILLY. (*Off L., as* WOMAN *laughs.*) Don't answer! Don't answer!

LETTA. (*At L. of* HAPPY *at exit.*) Don't you want to tell your father . . . ?

HAPPY. (*Pushes* LETTA *out.*) No, that's not my father. He's just a guy . . . Come on, we'll catch Biff, and, honey, we're going to paint this town! Stanley, where's the check! Hey, Stanley! (*They exit.* STANLEY *looks at L., then calls to* HAPPY.)

STANLEY. Mr. Loman! Mr. Loman! (*He picks up a chair and follows them off. Knocking is heard off L.* WOMAN *laughs off L. MUSIC CUE NO. 13.*)

84

WILLY. Will you stop laughing? Will you stop?

WOMAN. (*Enters* D. L., *crosses to* L. C. WILLY *follows her. She is dressed in a slip.*) Aren't you going to answer the door? He'll wake the whole hotel.

WILLY. I'm not expecting anybody. (*Putting on his vest. His collar is unbuttoned. He is carrying his coat. His tie is untied. Buttons cuffs on shirt.*)

WOMAN. Whyn't you go get yourself another drink, honey, and stop being so damn self-centered?

WILLY. I'm so lonely. (*Putting on vest.*)

WOMAN. You know you ruined me, Willy? You ruined me! From now on, whenever you come to the office, I'll see that you go right through to the buyers. You ruined me. (*Crosses to him. Hugs him.*)

WILLY. That's nice of you to say that.

WOMAN. Gee, you are self-centered! Why so sad? You are the saddest, self-centeredest soul I ever did see-saw. (*She laughs. Pulls him around and* L. *by his belt.*) Come on inside, drummer boy. It's silly to be dressing in the middle of the night. (*Knocking is heard.*) Aren't you going to answer the door?

WILLY. They're knocking on the wrong door. It's a mistake.

WOMAN. Then tell him to go away!

WILLY. There's nobody there. (*Knock.*)

WOMAN. It's getting on my nerves. There's somebody standing out there and it's getting on my nerves!

WILLY. (*Pushing her off. Worried.*) All right, stay in the bathroom here, and don't come out. I think there's a law in Massachusetts about it, so don't come out. It may be that new room clerk. He looked very mean. So don't come out. It's a mistake. (*Music fades out. Finally pushes her off* L. *Knocking is heard. He walks away* U. L.) Biff . . . (BIFF *enters past* WILLY. BIFF *has on sweater with " S " on it and three-fourth length raincoat.*)

BIFF. (*Crosses* D.) Why didn't you answer?

WILLY. (*Following him.*) Biff! What are you doing in Boston?

BIFF. (*At* L. C., *puts small suitcase* D.) Why didn't you answer? I've been knocking for five minutes, I called you on the phone . . .

WILLY. (*At* BIFF'S L.) I just heard you. I was in the bathroom and had the door shut. Did anything happen home?

BIFF. Dad . . . I let you down.

WILLY. What do you mean?

85

BIFF. Dad . . .

WILLY. Biffo, what's this about? (*Starts to pick up bag.*) Come on, let's go downstairs and get you a malted. . . .

BIFF. Dad, I flunked Math. (WILLY *stops.*)

WILLY. Not for the term.

BIFF. The term. I haven't got enough credits to graduate.

WILLY. (*Puts bag* D.) You mean to say Bernard wouldn't give you the answers?

BIFF. He did, he tried, but I only got a sixty-one.

WILLY. And they wouldn't give you four points?

BIFF. Birnbaum refused absolutely. I begged him, Pop, but he won't give me those points. You gotta talk to him before they close the school. Because if he saw the kind of man you are, and you just talked to him in your way . . . I'm sure he'd come through for me. The class came right before practice, see, and I didn't go enough. Would you talk to him? He'd like you, Pop. You know the way you could talk.

WILLY. You're on. We'll drive right back.

BIFF. Oh, Dad, good work! I'm sure he'll change it for you!

WILLY. (*Picks up suitcase, hands it to* BIFF. *They cross* U. *to entrance.*) Go downstairs and tell the clerk I'm checkin' out. Go right down.

BIFF. (*Crosses back few steps.*) Yes, sir! See, the reason he hates me, Pop . . . one day he was late for class so I got up at the blackboard and imitated him. . . . I crossed my eyes and talked with a lithp.

WILLY. (*Laughs.*) You did? The kids like it?

BIFF. They nearly died laughing!

WILLY. Yeah? What'd you do? (BIFF *crosses back* D., *puts suitcase* D., *stands straight.*)

BIFF. The thquare root of thixthy-twee is . . . (WILLY *bursts out laughing,* BIFF *joins him.*) And in the middle of it he walked in! (WILLY *laughs and* WOMAN *joins in, off.*)

WILLY. (*Without hesitation.*) Hurry downstairs and . . .

BIFF. Somebody in there?

WILLY. No, that was next door. . . . (*Picking up bag, giving it to* BIFF. WOMAN *laughs offstage.*)

BIFF. Somebody got in your bathroom!

WILLY. No, it's the next room, there's a party. . . .

WOMAN. (*Enters laughing,* WILLY'S *bathrobe around her shoul-*

86

ders. *Crosses to* L. *of* WILLY. *She lisps this.*) Can I come in? There's something in the bathtub, Willy, and it's *moving.* (WILLY *looks at* BIFF, *who is staring open-mouthed and horrified at* WOMAN.)

WILLY. (*Closes her bathrobe.*) Ah . . . you better go back to your room . . . they must be finished painting by now. They're painting her room so I let her take a shower here. Go back, go back. . . . (*Pushing her.*)

WOMAN. (*Resisting.*) But I've got to get dressed, Willy, I can't . . .

WILLY. Get out of here . . . go back, go back . . . (*Suddenly striving for the ordinary.*) This is Miss Francis, Biff, she's a buyer . . . they're painting her room. . . . Go back, Miss Francis, go back. . . .

WOMAN. But my clothes, I can't go out naked in the hall. . . .

WILLY. (*Pushes her off* L.) Get outa here! (*Follows her.*) Go back, go back!

WOMAN. (*Off* L.) Where's my stockings? You promised me stockings, Willy!

WILLY. (*Off stage.*) I have no stockings here! (BIFF *crosses* D. *few steps, sits on suitcase facing front.*)

WOMAN. (*Off.*) You had two boxes of size nine sheers for me and I want them!

WILLY. (*Off.*) Here, for God's sake, will you get outa here! (*He hands her a package. She enters, looking at stockings in box, followed by* WILLY *with her clothes.*)

WOMAN. (*Entering.*) You've certainly got your nerve, Willy. (*Taking her clothes from him.*) I just hope there's nobody in the hall. That's all I hope. (*Crosses to* L. *of* BIFF. *To* BIFF.) Are you football or baseball? (*Touching his hair.*)

BIFF. (*Pulling away.*) Football. . . .

WOMAN. (*Angry, humiliated.*) That's me too. G'night. (*She walks out* U. L. *A pause.*)

WILLY. (*Crosses to* L. *of* BIFF.) Well, better get going. I want to get to the school first thing in the morning. Get my suits out of the closet. . . . I'll get my valise. . . . (BIFF *hasn't moved.*) What's the matter? (BIFF *remains motionless, tears falling.*) She's a buyer. Buyer for J. H. Simmons. . . . She lives down the hall. . . . They're painting . . . You don't imagine . . . (*He breaks off. Pause.*) Now listen, pal, she's just a buyer. She sees merchandise in her room and they have to keep it looking just so . . . (*Pause. He assumes command.*) All right, get my suits. (BIFF *doesn't move.*) Now stop crying and do as I say. I gave you an order. Biff, I gave you an order! Is that what you do when I give you an order? How dare you cry! (WILLY *puts arm around him.*) Now look, Biff, when you grow up you'll understand about these things. You mustn't . . . you mustn't overemphasize a thing like this. I'll see Birnbaum first thing in the morning.

BIFF. Never mind.

WILLY. Never mind! He's going to give you those points. I'll see to it.

BIFF. He wouldn't listen to you.

WILLY. He certainly will listen to me. You need those points for the U. of Virginia.

BIFF. I'm not going there.

WILLY. Heh? . . . if I can't get him to change that mark you'll make it up in summer school. You've got all summer to . . .

BIFF. (*His weeping breaks from him.*) Dad . . .

WILLY. (*Infected by it. Kneels at L. of BIFF.*) Oh, my boy . . .

BIFF. Dad . . .

WILLY. (*Hugging BIFF.*) She's nothing to me, Biff, I was lonely, I was terribly lonely . . .

BIFF. You . . . you gave her Mama's stockings! (*His tears break through.*)

WILLY. (*Grabs him.*) I gave you an order!

BIFF. Don't touch me, you . . . liar! (*Rises.*)

WILLY. Apologize for that!

BIFF. You fake! You phoney little fake! You fake! (*Overcome, he turns quickly, and weeping fully, goes out with his valise, U. L. WILLY is left on floor on his knees.*)

WILLY. (*Shouting.*) I gave you an order! Biff, come back here or I'll beat you! Come back here! I'll whip you! (STANLEY *comes in from R., runs across L. and stands in front of him. WILLY shouts at him.*) I gave you an order . . . (*Other* WAITER *follows* STAN-LEY *in, stops above R. table, watching.*)

STANLEY. Hey, let's pick it up, pick it up, Mister Loman. (*He helps him to his feet.*) Your boys left. They said they'll see you home.

WILLY. But we were supposed to have dinner together.

STANLEY. (*Above him. Helping him on with his coat.*) Can you make it? (*MUSIC CUE NO.* 14.)

WILLY. I'll . . . sure, I can make it. (*Suddenly concerned about his clothes.*) Do I . . . I look all right?

STANLEY Sure, you look all right. (*Flicks a speck off his lapel.*)

WILLY. Here . . . here's a dollar.

STANLEY. Oh, your son paid me, it's all right.

WILLY. (*Putting it in his hand.*) No, take it. You're a good boy.

STANLEY. Ah, no, you don't have to . . .

WILLY. Here . . . here's some more. I don't need it any more. (*Crosses R. past STANLEY. Slight pause. STANLEY follows, puts money in WILLY's pocket.*) Tell me . . . is there a seed store in the neighborhood?

STANLEY. Seeds? You mean like to plant?

WILLY. (*At R. C.*) Yes. Carrots, peas . . . (*Other WAITER picks up WILLY's hat from under chair.*)

STANLEY. Well, there's hardware stores on Sixth Avenue, but it may be too late now.

WILLY. (*Anxiously.*) Oh, I'd better hurry. I've got to get some seeds. (*He starts off to R.*) I've got to get some seeds, right away. Nothing's planted. I don't have a thing in the ground. (*Music fades out. As he goes out U. R. WAITER gives him his hat. He hurries out. STANLEY moves over to R. after him, watches him off. Other WAITER stares at WILLY.*)

STANLEY. (*To WAITER.*) Well, whatta you looking at!? (*WAITER moves out, STANLEY follows him. Light fades on this. The light gradually rises on kitchen. It is empty. HAPPY appears at U. L. entrance, followed by BIFF. HAPPY wearing a hat, is carrying a large bunch of long-stemmed roses. Enters kitchen, looking for LINDA. Not seeing her, he turns to BIFF, who is just outside door, and makes a gesture with his hands, indicating, " not here, I guess." He crosses to bedroom door. LINDA enters from bathroom. He backs up. BIFF enters kitchen, closes door.*)

HAPPY. Heh, what're you doing up? (*She says nothing, but moves toward BIFF implacably.*) Where's Pop? Is he sleeping?

LINDA. Where were you?

HAPPY. (*Trying to laugh it off, crosses L. to her.*) We met two girls, Mom, very fine types. . . . Here, we brought you some flowers. . . . (*Offering them to her.*) Put them in your room, Ma. . . . (*She knocks them to floor at BIFF's feet.*) Now what'd

89

you do that for? (*Backs up few steps. She stares at* BIFF, *silent.*)
Mom, I want you to have some flowers. . . .
LINDA. (*Dressed in blue sweater and black dress. To* BIFF, *violently cutting* HAPPY *off.*) Don't you care whether he lives or dies?
HAPPY. (*Going to stairs.*) Come upstairs, Biff. . . .
BIFF. (*With flare of disgust.*) Leave me alone! (*To* LINDA.) What do you mean, lives or dies? Nobody's dying around here, pal.
LINDA. Get out of my sight! Get out of here!
BIFF. I wanna see the boss.
LINDA. You're not going near him!
BIFF. Where is he? (*He moves into the master bedroom sharply and then into bathroom.* LINDA *shouting after him.*)
LINDA. You invite him for dinner. He looks forward to it all day . . . and then you desert him there? There's no stranger you'd do that to!
HAPPY. Listen, when I desert him I hope I don't outlive the day!
LINDA. Get out of here!
HAPPY. Now look, Mom . . .
LINDA. Did you have to go to women tonight? You and your lousy rotten whores! (BIFF *re-enters kitchen. Crosses to* R. *of table.*)
HAPPY. Mom, all we did was follow Biff around—(*Indicating* BIFF.) trying to cheer him up! (*To* BIFF.) Boy, what a night you gave me!
LINDA. Get out of here, both of you, and don't come back! I don't want you tormenting him any more. Go on now, get your things together. (*To* BIFF.) You can sleep in his apartment. (*She starts to pick up flowers, stops herself.*) Pick up this stuff, I'm not your maid any more. Pick it up, you bum, you! (HAPPY *pushes hat forward over his eyes, turns his back to her in refusal, crosses* U. *to entrance to bedroom.* BIFF *slowly moves over* L., *and gets down on his knees, picking up flowers.*) You're a pair of animals! Not one, not another living soul would have had the cruelty to walk out on that man in a restaurant!
BIFF. (*Looking at her.*) Is that what he said?
LINDA. He didn't have to say anything. He was so humiliated he nearly limped when he came in.
HAPPY. But, Mom, he had a great time with us. . . .
BIFF. (*Cutting him off violently.*) Shut up! (*Without another*
90

word, HAPPY *goes upstairs. Takes off coat, lies on bed, changes to black tie.)*

LINDA. You! You didn't even go in to see if he was all right!?

BIFF. *(With self-loathing, he is still on floor in front of her, flowers in his hand.)* No . . . didn't. Didn't do a damned thing! How do you like that, heh? Left him babbling in a toilet.

LINDA. You louse. You . . .

BIFF. Right! Now you hit it right on the nose! *(He gets up, throws flowers in waste-basket, at* R. *of refrigerator.)* The scum of the earth, and you're looking at him!

LINDA. Get out of here!

BIFF. I gotta talk to the boss, Mom. Where is he?

LINDA. You're not going near him. Get out of this house!

BIFF. *(With absolute assurance, determination.)* No. We're gonna have an abrupt conversation, him and me. . . .

LINDA. You're not talking to him. . . . *(Hammering is heard from outside the house, off* R. BIFF *turns toward noise.* LINDA *is suddenly pleading.)* Will you please leave him alone?

BIFF. What's he doing out there?

LINDA. *(Broken-hearted.)* He's planting the garden!

BIFF. Now?! . . . Oh, my God! *(*BIFF *moves outside* L. *on to porch.* LINDA *following as* WILLY *from* U. R. *walks down* C. *carrying a flashlight, a hoe, and a handful of packets of seeds.)*

WILLY. *(Raps top of hoe he is carrying sharply to hold it firm.* BIFF *crosses out* U. L., *then* WILLY *moves from* R. *end of pit* L. *to* C. *measuring off distance with his foot. He holds flashlight to look at seed packets, reading off instructions.)* Carrots . . . quarter-inch apart; rows . . . one foot rows. *(He measures it off.)* One foot. *(Puts down package and measures off.)* Beets. *(Puts down another package and measures again.)* Lettuce . . . *(*LINDA *stands in door facing* L. WILLY *puts down package.)* One foot . . . *(Breaks off as* BEN *appears* U. R., *smoking cigarette, carrying umbrella, moves slowly down* R.)* What a proposition, ts, ts! . . . terrific, terrific! 'Cause she's suffered, Ben, the woman has suffered. You understand me? A man can't go out the way he came in, Ben, a man has got to add up to something. You can't, you can't . . . *(*BEN *moves toward him as though to interrupt.)* You gotta consider, now . . . don't answer so quick . . . remember, it's a guaranteed twenty-thousand dollar proposition. *(Crosses* R. *to* BEN. *Puts seeds in* L. *pants pocket.)* Now look, Ben, I want you

91

to go through the ins and outs of this thing with me. I've got no-body to talk to, Ben, and the woman has suffered, you hear me? (*Puts flashlight in* R. *pants pocket.*)

BEN. (*Arm around* WILLY'S *shoulder, now still, considering.*) What's the proposition?

WILLY. It's twenty thousand dollars on the barrelhead; guaranteed, gilt-edged, you understand?

BEN. You don't want to make a fool of yourself. They might not honor the policy.

WILLY. How can they dare refuse? Didn't I work like a coolie to meet every premium on the nose? And now they don't pay off? Impossible!

BEN. It's called a cowardly thing, William.

WILLY. Why? Does it take more guts to stand here the rest of my life ringing up a zero?

BEN. (*Yielding.*) That's a point, William. (*He moves* U. S., *thinking, turns.*) And twenty thousand . . . that is something one can feel with the hand, it is *there*.

WILLY. (*Now assured, with rising power. Kneels, puts hoe down, faces front, planting.* BEN *slowly crosses* D.) Oh, Ben, that's the whole beauty of it! I see it like a diamond, shining in the dark, hard and rough that I can pick up and touch in my hand. Not like . . . like an appointment! This would not be another damned-fool appointment, Ben, and it changes all the aspects; because he thinks I'm nothing, see, and so he spites me, but the funeral . . . (*Rises, straightens up now. With vengeance.*) Ben, that funeral will be massive! They'll come from Maine, Massachusetts, Vermont, New Hampshire . . . all the old-timers with the strange license plates—that boy will be thunderstruck, Ben, because he never realized—*I am known!* Rhode Island, New York, New Jersey—I am known, Ben, and he'll see it with his eyes once and for all; he'll see what I am, Ben! (*Crosses* R. *to edge of pit.*) He's in for a shock, that boy!

BEN. (*Coming to* R. *edge of garden.*) He'll call you a coward . . .

WILLY. (*Sudden fear.*) No, that would be terrible!

BEN. Yes. And a damned fool . . .

WILLY. No, no, he mustn't. I won't have that! (*He is broken and desperate.*)

BEN. He'll hate you, William. (*MUSIC CUE NO. 15.*)

WILLY. Oh, Ben, how do we get back to all the great times? Used to be so full of light, and comradeship, the sleigh-riding in winter, and the ruddiness on his cheeks; and always some kind of good news coming up, always something nice coming up ahead; and never even let me carry the valises in the house, and simonizing, simonizing that little red car! Why, why can't I give him something and not have him hate me?

BEN. (*Crosses* u. *to trellis by entrance* u. r.) Let me think about it. (*He glances at his watch.* WILLY *crosses* u. *a few steps.*) I still have a little time. Remarkable proposition, but you've got to be sure you're not making a fool of yourself. (*He has drifted off upstage and is out of sight.* BIFF *comes down from* L. *Music fades out.*)

BIFF. Pop . . .

WILLY. (*Suddenly conscious of* BIFF, *turns and looks at him, then crosses* D., *begins picking up packages of seeds in confusion. Moving from* C. *to* R. *end of pit.*) Where the hell is that seed? (*Indignantly.*) You can't see nothing out here, they boxed in the whole goddam neighborhood! (*Puts seeds in pocket.*)

BIFF. (*Crosses* D. *to* L. *of* WILLY. LINDA *stands on porch.*) I'm saying good-bye to you, Pop. (WILLY *looks at him, silent, unable to move.*) I'm not coming back any more.

WILLY. You're not going to see Oliver tomorrow?

BIFF. I've got no appointment, Dad.

WILLY. He put his arm around you and you've got no appointment?

BIFF. Pop, get this now, will you? Every time I've left it's been a fight that sent me out of here. Today I realized something about myself and I tried to explain it to you and I . . . I think I'm just not smart enough to make any sense out of it for you. To hell with whose fault it is or anything like that! (*He takes* WILLY'S *arm.*) Let's just wrap it up, heh? Come on in, we'll tell Mom. (*He gently tries to pull* WILLY *to* L.)

WILLY. (*With guilt.*) No, I don't want to see her.

BIFF. Come on. . . . (*He pulls again, but* WILLY *pulls away from him.*)

WILLY. (*Crosses* L. *below past* BIFF, *picks up hoe. With a high nervousness.*) No—no, I don't want to see her.

BIFF. (*Crosses above past* WILLY, *trying to stop him. Tries to look into* WILLY'S *face, as if to find the answer there.*) Why don't you want to see her?

WILLY. (*Crosses above past* BIFF. *More harshly now.*) Don't bother me, will you?

BIFF. (*At* R. *of* WILLY, *holding him by the arms. Shakes* WILLY. LINDA *crosses* D. *to* L. *of* WILLY.) What do you mean, you don't want to see her!? You don't want them calling you yellow, do you? This isn't your fault, it's me, I'm a bum. Now come inside. (WILLY *pulls against him, silent.* LINDA, *behind* WILLY, *puts hands on his arms.*)

LINDA. Did you plant, dear? (WILLY *pulls away and enters kitchen. She tries to follow him, but* BIFF *stops her in front of porch.* WILLY *crosses, puts hoe by door to bedroom, seeds, flashlight on shelf.*)

BIFF. (HAPPY *comes downstairs in his shirt sleeves.*) All right, we had it out. I'm going and I'm not writing any more.

LINDA. (*Going to* WILLY, *who has crossed to* D. R. *of kitchen.* BIFF *enters kitchen, closes door.*) I think that's the best way, dear. 'Cause there's no use drawing it out, you'll just never get along. (*She wipes his hand with her handkerchief.* WILLY *doesn't respond.* HAPPY *crosses to refrigerator.*)

BIFF. People ask where I am and what I'm doing, you don't know, and you don't care. That way it'll be off your mind and you can start brightening up again. All right? That clears it, doesn't it? (WILLY *is silent and* BIFF *goes to him, crossing below table.*) You gonna wish me luck, scout? (*Extends his hand.*) What do you say?

LINDA. (*Above* L. *of* WILLY.) Shake his hand, Willy.

WILLY. (*Turning to her, seething with hurt.*) There's no necessity to mention the pen at all, y' know. . . .

BIFF. (*Gently.*) I've got no appointment, Dad.

WILLY. (*Erupting fiercely.*) He put his arm around . . . ?

BIFF. Dad, you're never going to see what I am, so what's the use of arguing? If I strike oil I'll send you a check, meantime forget I'm alive.

WILLY. (*To* LINDA.) Spite, see?

BIFF. Shake hands, Dad.

WILLY. Not my hand.

BIFF. I was hoping not to go this way.

WILLY. Well, this is the way you're going. . . . Good-bye. (BIFF *looks at him a moment, then turns sharply and goes toward kitchen door.* WILLY *stops him with:*) May you rot in hell if you leave this house!

BIFF. (*Turning.*) Exactly what is it that you want from me!?

WILLY. (*Crosses to* R. *of table.* LINDA *crosses* U. R.) I want you to know, on the train, in the mountains, in the valleys, wherever you go, that you cut down your life for spite!

BIFF. No—no . . .

WILLY. Spite, spite, is the word of your undoing, and when you're down and out remember what did it. When you're rotting somewhere beside the railroad tracks, remember, and don't you dare blame it on me! . . .

BIFF. I'm not blaming it on you!

WILLY. I won't take the rap for this, you hear?

BIFF. That's just what I'm telling you!

WILLY. (*Sinking in chair* R. *of table.*) You're trying to put a knife in me, don't think I don't know what you're doing!

BIFF. (*Crosses to above table.*) All right, phoney! Then let's lay it on the line. (*He whips rubber tube out of his pocket, puts it on table.*)

LINDA. Biff! (*She moves to grab hose, but* BIFF *holds it down with his hand.*)

HAPPY. (*Crosses to* L. *of* BIFF.) You crazy!!

BIFF. Leave it there! Don't move it! (LINDA *above* R. *of* WILLY, *puts her arms around him.*)

WILLY. (*Doesn't look at it.*) What is that?

BIFF. You know goddamn well what that is.

WILLY. (*Caged, wanting to escape.*) I never saw that.

BIFF. You saw it, the mice didn't bring it into the cellar! What is this supposed to do, make a hero out of you? This supposed to make me sorry for you?

WILLY. Never heard of it.

BIFF. There'll be no pity for you, you hear it? No pity!

WILLY. (*To* LINDA. *Starts to rise.*) You hear the spite!

BIFF. (*Grabs* WILLY, *pushes him down.*) No, you're going to hear the truth, what you are and what I am!

LINDA. Stop it!!

WILLY. Spite!

HAPPY. You cut it now!

BIFF. (*To* HAPPY.) The man don't know who we are! The man is gonna know! (*To* WILLY.) We never told the truth for ten minutes in this house!

HAPPY. We always told the truth!

BIFF. (*Turning on him.*) You big blow, are you the assistant buyer? You're one of the two assistants to the assistant, aren't you?

HAPPY. Well, I'm practically . . .

BIFF. You're practically full of it, we all are! And I'm through with it. (*To* WILLY.) Now hear this, Willy, this is me.

WILLY. I know you!

BIFF. You know why I had no address for three months? I stole a suit in Kansas City and I was in jail. (LINDA *sobs, turns* U. S.) Stop crying. I'm through with it. (*She turns away from them, hands on her face.*)

WILLY. I suppose that's my fault!

BIFF. I stole myself out of every good job since high school!

WILLY. And whose fault is that!?

BIFF. And I never got anywhere because you blew me so full of hot air I could never stand taking orders from anybody! That's whose fault it is!

WILLY. I hear that!

LINDA. Don't, Biff.

BIFF. It's goddam time you heard that! I had to be boss big shot in two weeks, and I'm through with it!

WILLY. (*Rises, crosses* D. *to* D. R. *corner of kitchen.*) Then hang yourself; for spite, hang yourself!

BIFF. (*Putting tube in his pocket, crosses* D. *to* L. *of* WILLY.) No! Nobody's hanging himself, Willy! I ran down eleven flights with a pen in my hand today . . . and suddenly I stopped, you hear me? And in the middle of that office building . . . I saw . . . do you hear this!—I stopped in the middle of that building and I saw . . . the sky. I saw the things that I love in this world; the work and the food and time to sit and smoke. And I looked at the pen and said to myself what the hell am I grabbing this for? Why am I trying to become what I don't want to be? What am I doing in an office building making a contemptuous, begging fool of myself, when all I want is out there, waiting for me the minute I say I know who I am! Why can't I say that, Willy! (*He tries to turn* WILLY *to him to face him, but* WILLY *pulls away and moves to* L., *with hatred and threat.*)

WILLY. (*Crossing below table to* L. *end of kitchen.*) The door of your life is wide open!

BIFF. (*Crosses to* R. *of table.*) Pop! I'm a dime a dozen and so are you!

WILLY. (*At* L. *of kitchen. Turning on him now in an uncontrolled outburst.*) I am not a dime a dozen! I am Willy Loman, and you are Biff Loman!

BIFF. (*Crosses above toward* WILLY, *but* HAPPY *grabs him above table.*) I'm one dollar an hour, Willy! I tried seven states and couldn't raise it. A buck an hour, do you gather my meaning? I am not a leader of men, Willy, and neither are you; you were never anything but a hard working drummer who landed in the ashcan like all the rest of them! I'm not bringing home any prizes any more and you're going to stop waiting for me to bring them home!

WILLY. (*To his face now.*) You vengeful, spiteful mutt! (BIFF *breaks away from* HAPPY *and goes for* WILLY, *who goes to stairs to escape, but* BIFF *grabs him and pulls him around, shaking him.*)

BIFF. (*At the peak of his fury, shaking him.*) Pop, I'm nothing, I'm nothing, Pop! Can't you understand that? There's no spite in it any more. I'm just what I am, that's all. . . . (*His fury has spent itself and he breaks down, sobbing, holding on to* WILLY, *who takes him in his arms, comforting.*)

WILLY. What're you doing? What're you doing? (*To* LINDA.) Why is he crying?

BIFF. (*Crying, broken.*) Will you let me go, for Christ's sake? Will you take that phoney dream and burn it before something happens? (*Struggling to contain himself, he pulls away and moves to stairs.*) I'll go in the morning. Put him . . . put him to bed. . . . (*In exhaustion he moves out, upstairs to his room.*)

WILLY. (*Astonished, elevated.*) Isn't that . . . isn't that remarkable? Biff! He likes me!

LINDA. (*Above table.*) He loves you, Willy!

HAPPY. (U. S. *in kitchen, deeply moved.*) Always did, Pop.

WILLY. Oh . . . Biff! (*He is staring wildly.*) He cried! Cried to me! (*He is choking with his love, and now cries out his promise.*) That boy . . . that boy is going to be . . . magnificent! (BEN *appears in light just outside kitchen at* R.)

BEN. Yes, outstanding, with twenty thousand behind him. (*MUSIC CUE NO. 15A.*)

97

LINDA. (*She senses the racing of his mind—fearfully, carefully.*) Now come to bed, Willy. It's all settled now.

WILLY. (*He is finding it difficut not to rush out of house. Crosses below table to* D. R. *of kitchen.*) Yes, we'll sleep, come on . . . go to sleep, Hap. (LINDA *crosses to* HAPPY.)

BEN. Yes, and it does take a great kind of a man to crack the jungle. (LINDA *takes* HAPPY *to stairs.*)

HAPPY. (*Arm around* LINDA.) I'm getting married, Pop, don't forget it. I'm changing everything. I'm gonna run that department before the year is up. You'll see, Mom. . . . (*He kisses her.*)

BEN. The jungle is dark and full of diamonds, Willy. (WILLY *turns, moves to* D. S. *point of kitchen, listening to* BEN.)

LINDA. Be good. Go on up, dear.

HAPPY. 'Night, Pop. (*Goes upstairs.*)

LINDA. (*To* WILLY.) Come, dear. (*At above table, to* WILLY.)

BEN. (*Turns to* WILLY. *With greater force.*) One must go in to fetch a diamond out. (*Music fades out.*)

WILLY. (*He goes to her at* U. R. *of table.*) I just want to get settled down, Linda, let me sit alone for a little.

LINDA. (*At* WILLY'S L., *almost uttering her fear.*) I want you upstairs.

WILLY. (*As conscious that this is the last, loving good-bye, takes her in his arms.*) In a few minutes, Linda. I couldn't sleep right now. Go on, you look awful tired.

BEN. (*Standing with* R. *hand on umbrella.*) Not like an appointment at all, a diamond is rough, and hard to the touch.

WILLY. Go on now. I'll be right up.

LINDA. I think this is the only way, Willy.

WILLY. Sure, it's the best thing.

BEN. Best thing.

WILLY. Everything is gonna be . . . Go on, kid, get to bed. (*Kisses her.*) You look so tired.

LINDA. Come right up.

WILLY. Two minutes. (*She goes into the bedroom and sits on chair.* WILLY *moves to just outside kitchen door.*) Loves me. (*Wondrous.*) Always loved me. Isn't that a remarkable thing? Ben, he'll worship me for it!

BEN. (*With promise.*) It's dark there, but full of diamonds.

WILLY. Can you imagine that magnificence with twenty thousand dollars in his pocket?

LINDA. (*Rises and crosses* U. *to bedroom door—from her room, calling.*) Willy!? Come up!

WILLY. (*Calling into kitchen.*) Yes! Yes. . . . Coming! It's very smart, you realize that, don't you, sweetheart? Even Ben sees it. . . . 'Bye! (*Gently throws her a kiss. Closes door. Crosses* D. *to* L. C. *of stage.* LINDA *sits chair in bedroom.*) Imagine? When the mail comes he'll be ahead of Bernard *again!*

BEN. A perfect proposition all around.

WILLY. Did you see how he cried to me? (*Crosses* U. *toward house.*) Oh, if I could kiss him, Ben!

BEN. Time, William, time! (WILLY *stops.*)

WILLY. (*At* C.) Oh, Ben, I always knew one way or another we were gonna make it, Biff and I!

BEN. The boat. We'll be late. (*Moves slowly to* U. R. *exit.*)

WILLY. (*Backs away* D. C., *facing house.*) Now when you kick off, boy, I want a seventy-yard boot, and get right down the field under the ball and when you hit, hit low and hit hard, because it's important, boy, there's all kinds of important people in the stands—(*Turns front.*) and the first thing you know . . . (BEN *exits. Suddenly* WILLY *realizes he is alone.*) Ben! Ben, where do I . . . ? (*Makes a sudden movement of search.*) Ben, how do I . . . ? (*Crosses* L.)

LINDA. (*Rises—calling upstage.*) Willy, you coming up!!!!

WILLY. Sssssh!! (*He turns around as if to find his way, and moves* R. *MUSIC CUE NO. 16.*)

LINDA. Willy? (*As music rises,* WILLY *rushes off* U. R. *Music stops. No answer. She waits.* LINDA, *with real embodied fear.*) Willy, answer me! . . . Willy! (*MUSIC CUE NO. 16A. There is the sound of a car—car door slams—starting and moving away at full speed. Car rushes away. Loud crash of car.*) No!!! (LINDA *kneels on bed looking out of window.*)

HAPPY and BIFF. (*Rush to head of stairs.*) Pop!! (*As music changes* LINDA *exits. Boys cross to their beds, put on coats with black arm bands. They already have on black ties.* CHARLEY and BERNARD *enter from* U. L., *cross* D. *Knock on kitchen door, then they enter.* BERNARD *and* CHARLEY *are wearing dark blue double-breasted suits, and black ties.* CHARLEY *enters first, crosses to* L. *of table.* BERNARD *follows, closes door, crosses to* D. L. *of kitchen.* HAPPY *and* BIFF *come downstairs.* HAPPY *crosses to below bathroom door.* BIFF *stays on stairs.* LINDA *enters from bathroom wearing veil, black dress and gloves, and carrying a wreath. She looks at boys, then crosses to* CHARLEY. *The boys exchange a look. She takes* CHARLEY'S *arm and they all walk forward through kitchen to* D. C. LINDA *moves forward, places wreath* D. C. *She then sits down* C. *They all move as she sits.* BERNARD *moves* L. *and a few feet up,* CHARLEY *stays just to* L. *and above* LINDA. HAPPY *and* BIFF *look at each other, then move.* HAPPY *moves to* L. *of* CHARLEY. BIFF *moves few feet* R. *and above.)*

REQUIEM

CHARLEY. It's getting dark, Linda. (LINDA *doesn't react, staring at grave which is downstage above footlights* R. *of* C.)

BIFF. How about it, Ma? Better get some rest. They'll be closing the gate soon. (*But she makes no move.*)

HAPPY. (*As if defending himself against an accusation.*) He had no right to do that. There was no necessity for it. We would've helped him.

CHARLEY. (*Grunting.*) H'mmm.

BIFF. Come along, Mom.

LINDA. (*Pause.*) Why didn't anybody come?

CHARLEY. It was a very nice funeral.

BIFF. (*Crosses* D. *a step.*) It's almost night, Ma.

LINDA. I can't understand it. At this time, especially. First time in thirty-five years we were just about free and clear. He only needed a little salary. He was even finished with the dentist.

CHARLEY. (*To* LINDA.) No man only needs a little salary.

LINDA. I can't understand it.

BIFF. (*Comforting* LINDA.) There were a lot of nice days. When he'd come home from a trip; or on Sundays, making the stoop; finishing the cellar; putting on the new porch; when he built the extra bathroom; and put up the garage. . . . You know something, Charley, there's more of him in that front stoop than in all the sales he ever made.

CHARLEY. Yeah. . . . He was a happy man with a batch of cement.

LINDA. (*Still dazed.*) He was so wonderful with his hands.

BIFF. He had the wrong dreams. All, all wrong.

HAPPY. Don't say that.

BIFF. He never knew who he was.

100

HAPPY. That's an insult. (CHARLEY *grabs his arm, stops him.*)
CHARLEY. Nobody dast blame this man. You don't understand;
(*Crosses to* BIFF.) Willy was a salesman; and for a salesman,
there is no rock bottom to the life. He don't put a bolt to a nut,
he don't tell you the law, or give you medicine. He's a man way
out there in the blue, riding on a smile and a shoeshine; and
when they start not smiling back—boy, that's an earthquake. And
then you get yourself a couple of spots on your hat, and you're
finished. Nobody dast blame this man. A salesman is got to dream,
boy; it comes with the territory.
BIFF. Charley, the man never knew who he was. (CHARLEY *turns
away.*) Why don't you come with me, Happy?
HAPPY. I'm not licked that easily. I'm staying right in this city,
and I'm gonna beat this racket! . . . (*He looks at* BIFF, *his chin
set.*) The Loman Brothers!
BIFF. I know who I am, kid.
HAPPY. All right, boy. I'm gonna show you and everybody else
that Willy Loman did not die in vain. He had a good dream; it's
the only dream you can have. To come out number one man. He
fought it out here, and this is where I'm gonna win it for him.
BIFF. (*Squats* L. *of* LINDA.) Let's go, Mom.
LINDA. I'll be with you in a minute. Go on, Charley. (*He hesitates.*) I want to, just a minute. (CHARLEY *crosses* U. *to* L. *of table
that is* L. *of trellis entrance.* BERNARD *crosses to below table.*
HAPPY *crosses to above table.*) I never had a chance to say
good-bye. (BIFF *rises, remains a slight distance up and* L. *of*
LINDA. *She sits there, summoning herself.*) Forgive me, dear. I
can't cry. I don't understand it; I can't cry. It seems to me that
you're just on another trip. I keep expecting you. Willy, dear,
why did you do it? I search and search and I search, and I can't
understand it, Willy. I made the last payment on the house today.
Today, dear. And there'll be nobody home. (*MUSIC CUE NO.
17. Now a sob rises in her.*) We're free and clear. . . . (*Sobbing more fully, released.*) We're free. . . . (BIFF *comes slowly
to her* L.) We're free. . . . We're free. . . . (*Lifts her to her
feet and moves out up* R. *with her in his arms quietly sobbing.*
BERNARD *and* CHARLEY *come together and follow them, followed
by* HAPPY. *Only music of the flute is left on the darkening stage
as:*)

CURTAIN

101

PROPERTY PLOT

ACT I

Kitchen:
Sewing basket, threaded needles, silk stocking, cigarettes, matches and ashtray on refrigerator
Inside refrigerator: Cheese, bread, knife on top shelf. Milk, butter, etc., on other shelves
Ashtray on handrail
Table (26" x 18") covered with oilcloth
Three (3) chairs
Small refrigerator (30" x 48")
Small two-burner gas stove
Waste-basket
Telephone on stand
Knocker on kitchen door

Bedroom (downstairs):
Willy's slippers under bed
Bed (5½' x 3')
Small chair
Hairpins under pillow (Linda)

Boys' Bedroom:
Shoulder guards, old deflated football, battered football helmet, old sweater, etc., inside chest
Happy's hat on hook on bedroom wall
Double bunk
Two (2) pennants (u. of Ill. and u. of Ind.) on D. s. end of bunk
Pants hanging on hook
Chest (26" x 18" x 18")
Small can of water above chest (to be used as ashtray)
Rubber tubing under heater

Behind House:
Light brown sweater with large " S " (Biff)
Blue pajamas (Willy)
Sneakers (Biff)
Sneakers (Happy)
Housedress; rose colored rayon cotton print (Linda)
Apron; lavender-flowered (Linda)
Shoes; black suede, flat heels (Linda)
Hair ribbon; rose colored (Linda)
Stockings (Linda)
Basket of clean wash

Stage L.:
Woman's hat, scarf, suitjacket on hook on second portal
Megaphone (Woman, used for offstage voice)

Stage R.:
Two heavy worn sample cases (Willy)
Punching bag (Happy)
Alligator valise (Ben)
Umbrella (Ben)
Football (Biff)
Bucket with chamois (Happy)
Cigarettes and holder (Ben)

Hand Props:
Keys (Willy)
Pad and pencil in apron (Linda)
Deck of cards, cough drops, handkerchief (Charley)
Cigarettes and matches in pajamas, old-fashioned pocket watch (Happy)

102

At End of Act I—Strike:
Bread, cheese and knife

Kitchen:
Coffee on stove
Bread on table,
Cup and saucer on table
Willy's hat on chair L. of table
Willy's coat on chair by phone

Boys' Bedroom:
Arm bands on bunk

Behind House:
Wreath
Six (6) pennants (S. H. S.) on sticks
Wash basket
Black dress (Linda)
Long black gloves (Linda)
Black hat with veil (Linda)
Handkerchief (Linda)
Sweater; old blue cardigan (Linda)
Cloth coat; worn, outdated (Linda)
Brown hat; worn, outdated (Linda)

Restaurant—BERNARD's Office:
Table (24" x 20") with juke box lamp on u. s. shelf
Menu (on u. s. shelf)
Tablecloth for table that is brought on (on u. s. shelf)
Ashtray attached to table u. s. (water in ashtray)
Three (3) napkins on u. s. shelf
Ashtray on u. s. shelf, also matches
Chair

Stage L.:
Wire recorder (ashtray with cigar on it)

Happy's hat to stage L.
Make beds

ACT II

Football shoulder pads; pants; helmet, gold colored (pants stuffed with football shoes, towels, underwear, etc.)
Two boxes silk stockings (Woman)
Eight (8) roses
Suitcase (Biff)
Megaphone (Woman)
Sweater with large "S" on it (Biff)
Raincoat; three-fourth length, light colored (Biff)
Typewriter desk (26¾" x 16") for wire recorder, and chair

Stage R.:
Two tennis rackets (Bernard)
Valise (Bernard)
Bottle of bourbon (Charley)
Flashlight, 6 packages of seeds and hoe (Willy)
Alligator valise, and umbrella (same as Act I—Ben)
Table and 3 chairs (table 21½" x 20")
One glass champagne and three (3) double Scotches (Stanley)
Tray (Stanley)

Hand Props:
Cigarettes in handbag (Forsythe)
Address book in handbag (Forsythe)
Lighter (Howard)
Money in wallet (Charley)
Gold fountain pen (Biff)
Pocket watch (Ben)
Cigarette case (Bernard)
Cigars, pencils in vest (Charley)
Rubber tubing (Biff)
Stenographer's pad and pencil (Jennie)

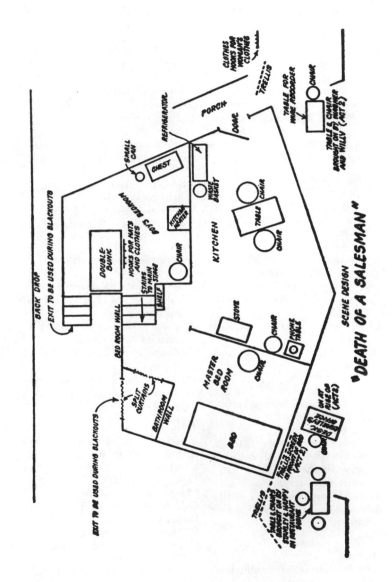

"DEATH OF A SALESMAN"

SCENE DESIGN